Differentiated Professional Development

in a *Professional Learning Community*

Linda Bowgren

Kathryn Sever

Solution Tree | Press

a division of
Solution Tree

555 North Morton Street
Bloomington, IN 47404
800.733.6786 (toll free) / 812.336.7700
FAX: 812.336.7790

email: info@solution-tree.com
solution-tree.com

Printed in the United States of America

13 12 11 10 09   1 2 3 4 5

FSC
Mixed Sources
Product group from well-managed
forests and other controlled sources

Cert no. SW-COC-002283
www.fsc.org
© 1996 Forest Stewardship Council

Library of Congress Cataloging-in-Publication Data

Bowgren, Linda.
  Differentiated professional development in a professional learning community /
Linda Bowgren, Kathryn Sever.
      p. cm.
  Includes bibliographical references and index.
  ISBN 978-1-934009-61-1 (perfect bound) -- ISBN 978-1-935249-27-6
(library binding) 1. Teachers--In-service training. 2. Teachers--Professional
relationships. 3. Professional learning communities. I. Sever, Kathryn. II.
Title.
  LB1731.B69 2010
  370.71'55--dc22
                                    2009030276

Solution Tree
Jeffrey C. Jones, CEO & President

Solution Tree Press
President: Douglas M. Rife
Publisher: Robert D. Clouse
Director of Production: Gretchen Knapp
Managing Production Editor: Caroline Wise
Senior Production Editor: Risë Koben
Indexer: Appingo
Proofreader: Rachel Rosolina
Text and Cover Designer: Amy Shock
Compositor: Quick Sort India Private Ltd.

For Joshua, Lauren, and Jeremiah—my greatest teachers!
With hugs and love,

Gram/NaNa

To "Team Sever," with love and gratitude for strength
on the journey!

—Kathy

Acknowledgments

We are blessed with many wonderful friends and family members who have supported us in this venture. We have needed and appreciated the encouragement of others and wish to thank and acknowledge:

Our colleagues in the Maine-Endwell Central School District, especially those learning leaders, teachers, and administrators who believe passionately in the power of differentiated job-embedded professional learning. This is your story and your challenge to continue.

Rick and Becky DuFour and all of the many educators who have provided resources and research not only for this book but also for our professional practice.

All of the wonderful people at Solution Tree! Special thanks to Gretchen Knapp and Risë Koben; we could not have been more fortunate in having two such talented and caring editors. We feel that we have found two new friends.

Our "informal editor," Joe Sever, who pored over many versions of each new chapter, sharing not only his professional expertise as an educator but also his encouragement to keep moving forward.

Alicia Boyce and Michele Doig, who have been conference co-presenters and constant cheerleaders. Thanks for your unyielding support and friendship.

From Linda:

The running of a marathon appears to be an individual accomplishment, but anyone who has done it knows it takes many behind-the-scenes trainers, coaches, family members, and friends to move the individual runner across time to the finish line. So it is with writing a book. As you hold this book in your hands, know that you hold the collaborative work of many of my colleagues, mentors, coaches, family members, and friends.

I begin by thanking my co-writer and friend, Kathy Sever. You were right. We can write a book!

"Thank you for your support" seems a woefully inadequate phrase to offer the Vestal Central School District's first professional development team. We were a true collaborative team, and our day-to-day interaction gave me ideas and immense pride in my profession. So, thank you to Marcia Modlo, Louise Cleveland, Christine Winterstein, Anne Panko, Sheri Serfass, Jane Hashey, Carey Gorgrant, and Michelle Wolf for teaching me, encouraging me, and always making me laugh. Most of all, my admiration and love go to my protégé, Sarah Evans. What an inspiration you are for this brilliant profession of teaching. See you at the finish line!

Enormous thanks to all the new teachers in the Maine-Endwell Central School District who so willingly accepted me as their mentor. Your enthusiasm, knowledge, and friendship made my last years of teaching truly enjoyable. My special thanks go to the dedicated K–12 literacy team, who supported me from the very beginning.

Likewise, thank you to my colleagues (every single pioneer, settler, and outlaw) in the Windsor Central School District for trusting me and sharing your time and students. I look forward to our continued collaboration. Your professional learning community is a pleasure to watch as it grows and strengthens.

Finally, eternal thanks go to my incredible family. To Mom and Dad, my most important teachers; my daughter, Carrie, my first and best collaborator; my son, Tyson, for believing in his mother's wisdom and strength; Rosemary, for loving my son so very much; my sister, Sharon, the touchstone of my life; my brother, Tom, for being proud of me; and of course my three grandchildren, Josh, LJ, and Jeremiah, who bring sheer joy to me every single day. And a very special thanks to Carole, whose support for my writing has always helped me find peace in my life.

From Kathy:

What an exciting beginning to retirement! Instead of ending a career, we are embarking on a new journey as authors. I will always remember 2009 as a year of both challenge and celebration.

Our family faced a significant challenge when my husband was struck with Guillain-Barre syndrome. Joe's inner strength, perseverance, and faith have been an inspiration. We have been blessed with the prayers and support of family, friends, and colleagues: "Team Sever." Please know that we appreciate each and every one of you!

I would like to thank my family, especially:

My parents, Olive and Donald Skinner. You sacrificed to give my brother Jon and me a loving family life, summers at the lake, and an education. From childhood, you told me that you chose a name for me that would look good on a book. So here it is, just for you: Kathryn Don Skinner.

My husband, Joe. When you meet in a castle in France, it crosses your mind that life may never get better than this. But it has. You are my best friend, my mentor, and my true love. Thank you for supporting me through life's challenges. I am looking forward to many years of walking on the beach together. *Je t'aime.*

My "bonus children," Joe, Matt, and Brenda, and their wonderful families. What a gift you are in my life!

My son, Kyle. The expression may be a cliché, but you are truly my "pride and joy." Being your mom is such a blessing! Every moment since you were born has been richer for having you in my life. Thank you for your encouragement during the writing of this book! It has kept me going. My love and support go with you always.

My professional life has been shaped by interactions with many wonderful educators too numerous to mention. It is with special appreciation that I acknowledge:

Ed Babino and Whit Garland, who hired me for my first teaching position.

Dave Stark, who supervised my administrative internship.

Connie Lorden, who hired me for my first administrative position.

Al Guzzi, who through his example taught me that the best decisions are those based on principles.

Jack Touhey, who always based his decisions on the best interests of children and made it possible for me to balance my roles as a mom and as a professional leader.

Gary Worden, who brought the book *Professional Learning Communities at Work* to Maine-Endwell.

Pat Kubik, Carol Weber, and Ginny Spencer, who supported me through so many tasks and challenges!

And thanks to my friend and co-author, Linda. Writing this book together has been *fun*. Here's to more laughter and learning as the journey continues!

Solution Tree Press would like to thank the following reviewers:

Rebecca DuFour
Educational Consultant, Presenter, and Author
Moneta, Virginia

Karen M. Dyer
Group Director
Center for Creative Leadership
Greensboro, North Carolina

Parry Graham
Principal
Lufkin Road Middle School
Apex, North Carolina

Stephanie Hirsh
Executive Director
National Staff Development Council
Dallas, Texas

Tamara Honvlez
Director of Curriculum and Staff Development
Litchfield Elementary School District #79
Litchfield Park, Arizona

Jane Kise
Educational Consultant and Author
Minneapolis, Minnesota

Claudette Rasmussen
Senior Professional Development Associate
Learning Point Associates
Chicago, Illionis

Rick Wormeli
Educational Consultant and Author
Herndon, Virginia

Table of Contents

CHAPTER 6
Responsibility and Use: "You Do"

CHAPTER 7
Teacher Leaders as Mentors and Team Facilitators

CHAPTER 8
Time Out!

CHAPTER 9
Ten Principles for Principals

CHAPTER 10

About the Authors

 **Linda Bowgren** has been an educator since 1965, serving in both private and public schools as a high school physical education teacher and coach, an elementary classroom teacher, and a literacy specialist/professional developer. She received her master of science degree in literacy from Elmira College, New York. Linda retired in 2008 from the Maine-Endwell Central School District in Endwell, New York, where she worked to develop the new-teacher induction program and served as the district's new-teacher mentor. She currently enjoys working as a consultant in districts interested in revisiting literacy and professional development methods and practices. Linda has presented at many state and national conferences on the topics of literacy, instructional strategies, and professional development and is a firm believer in collaboration and building a culture of professionalism for all teachers. She lives in Endicott, New York, in happy proximity to her three young grandchildren. Her retirement offers many opportunities for sharing books, biking, camping, canoeing, gardening, and tree-house construction.

 **Kathryn Sever** has been a public school educator since 1974. She has served as a classroom teacher, building administrator, and director of education. Before retiring in 2009, she was assistant superintendent for instruction in the Maine-Endwell Central School District in Endwell, New York. Kathy holds a bachelor's

degree in French from Bates College (1970) and both a master's degree in French and a master of education degree in curriculum and instruction from the University of Hawaii at Manoa (1973). She has presented at several local, state, and national conferences. Kathy resides in Endwell, New York, with her husband, Joe—whom she met in a castle in France when they were both French teachers traveling and studying under Rotary Club sponsorship. Their son, Kyle, graduated from Fordham University in 2009.

Linda and Kathy are the coauthors of "Shaping the Workday," which appears in the anthology *Finding Time for Professional Learning* (2008).

Introduction

Today, when we speak of professional development, we use terms such as *collaboration, learning teams, peer coaching, team leaders,* and *lead teachers.* Carol Lyons and Gay Su Pinnell (2001, p. 184) describe professional development as "the ways people engage in learning so that they build commitment and ownership, and form a community with shared meanings." Laura Robb (2000, p. 19) views schools as "centers of inquiry, where teachers and administrators pose questions, pinpoint problems, study, reflect, and collaborate to discover possible answers." The National Staff Development Council (2009a, home-page) is committed to the proposition that student learning needs should define educators' learning needs and that professional development should "foster collective responsibility for improved student performance." Thomas Guskey (2000, p. 16) refers to professional development as an "intentional, ongoing, and systematic process." Current definitions of professional development are sounding less like inservice training and more like the actual process of learning.

Indeed, districts that have adopted the principles of professional learning communities "operate under the assumption that the key to improved learning for students is continuous, job-embedded learning for educators" (DuFour, DuFour, & Eaker, 2008, p. 14). What, then, is the key to successful learning for educators? We believe that it is *differentiating* instruction for teacher learners. Differentiating professional development guarantees that teachers can and will engage in job-embedded learning as part of their daily work habits.

At the outset, we must stress that "differentiating" does not mean supporting individuals' personal interests and agendas. To the contrary, the goal of differentiating the delivery of professional development for individual adult learners is to support the mission of the professional learning community. Richard DuFour, Rebecca DuFour, and Robert Eaker (2008, p. 14) define a professional learning community as *"educators committed to working collaboratively in ongoing processes of collective inquiry and action research to achieve better results for the students they serve."* Differentiation makes it possible for teachers to work interdependently on collaborative teams that focus on student learning, rather than teaching, to support the learning of all students.

This book will make it clear that differentiating professional development affects four areas of a school culture:

1. The way that time is used within the workday

2. The structure of the workday for staff members

3. The variety of professional development models that are available

4. The support offered to teachers by administrators and colleagues

When districts find the right formula whereby each of these four components affects and is affected by the others, they can produce a system of learning for everyone.

The Basics of Differentiation

Differentiation is not just about the *how* of learning. *Who* the learner is defines and influences the course of learning. Confucius recognized that all learners differ in their readiness. When teaching, one must begin where the learner is and build upon what is known. All students come to the world of learning with a set of individualized characteristics, likes, dislikes, and life experiences. Teachers recognize that all students are different and that those differences illuminate the way for the teaching. Carol Ann Tomlinson and Caroline Cunningham Eidson (2003) explain that when we combine whom we teach with what we teach, where we teach, and how we teach, we engage in *responsive teaching*. Deep learning results when a teacher understands each student, develops an appreciation for the values students place on the learning process, and responds to individual needs.

Many researchers, beginning with Carl Jung (1923/1974), have studied *learning styles* in an effort to help educators increase learning outcomes for students. Harvey Silver, Richard Strong, and Matthew Perini (2007) have identified four distinct types of learners: mastery learners, understanding learners, self-expressive learners, and interpersonal learners. Mastery learners need models, practice, and feedback in their effort to learn practical information. Understanding learners are curious and hunger to debate issues. Self-expressive learners are creative and like to use their imagination to explore new ideas. Interpersonal learners succeed when the focus is on building personal relationships and community. In *The Strategic Teacher*, Silver, Strong, and Perini note that "teaching strategies also have styles" (2007, p. 6). When instructors become familiar with and fully understand the implications of matching teaching strategies to the learning styles in the room, it becomes possible to develop an effective framework for differentiation. Teachers hope to motivate all students by addressing their preferred styles. At the same time, teachers can help students to develop new learning skills through the challenge of working within all four learning styles (Silver et al., 2007).

Much has been written about the value, necessity, and complexity of differentiating learning within every classroom based on student readiness, motivation and interest, apparent skills, learning preferences or styles, and identified cognitive needs. Teachers are encouraged to look at differentiation for students not as a formula for teaching, but rather as a way of thinking about and shaping the learning experiences of all (Tomlinson & Strickland, 2005). If, as Robert Marzano, Debra Pickering, and Jane Pollock note in their book *Classroom Instruction That Works* (2001), the classroom teacher is the most important factor in student success, then how can we ignore the value of differentiation for the most valuable students: our teachers themselves?

The teacher as the most valuable student.

Professional development experiences are planned for the purpose of helping teachers fill their "toolbox" with a variety of teaching strategies. Responsive teaching of adults brings the realization that one-size-fits-all professional development cannot provide success for all. Just as classroom teachers are challenged to meet the needs of the diverse learning styles of their students, professional development specialists need to incorporate learning styles into their work with adult learners. While teacher learners are not limited to one learning style, they typically rely on the one that is the most comfortable and best developed. Every teacher trainer must also be prepared to overcome teachers' barriers to learning and must be able to provide appropriate adult motivation. Matching teacher needs with district initiatives requires adjustments in planning and implementing professional development activities. Differentiation is key!

A Cultural Shift

DuFour, DuFour, and Eaker stress that "it is impossible for a school or district to develop the capacity to function as a professional learning community without undergoing profound cultural shifts" (2008, p. 91). Differentiation of professional learning for teachers is one such profound shift. Districts must gradually and systematically move from the one-shot, one-day, out-of-the-district workshop to job-embedded, teacher-led collaboration in which everyone's learning style can be consciously considered.

When professional development has a top-down design, building needs, department needs, grade-level needs, and certainly individual teacher needs may not be addressed. How often have we heard about, or felt, a disconnect between our professional needs and the workshops that we are required to attend on conference days? "Why do I have to go to this?" "What does this have to do with what I teach?" These questions resonate throughout the halls of many schools today. While teachers may actually find a certain comfort in the fact that the traditional, large-group workshop model seldom requires any action or engagement, it is rare that a one-size-fits-all workshop really does "fit all," and rarer still that it leads to increased student achievement back in the classroom. Yet it is the moral responsibility of all teachers to improve every student's chances of success. The answer is to use data interpretation to drive differentiated professional development for schools, grade levels, and individual teachers. When teams of teachers engage in the interpretation of student data, they are able to generate solutions to achievement gaps. When school cultures use data as a means to an end, academic interventions for individual students are set in motion.

Differentiation in Practice

This book is intended to be a resource for educators who are interested in sustaining the development of their professional learning communities by establishing differentiation as a model that ensures both teacher and student achievement. Our goal is to share research and strategies that will assist readers in supporting targeted differentiated professional learning in their own districts.

Chapter 1 explores differentiation in more detail and looks at the connections between differentiation and collaborative learning.

Chapter 2 summarizes the relevant theories of adult learning and introduces the research-based three-step model of professional development that we call "I Do, We Do, You Do." As they implement this model, the leaders of professional development engage in a *gradual release of responsibility* for learning. The responsibility transfers from the leaders, who begin the process by demonstrating new strategies, to the teachers, who ultimately apply those strategies in their classrooms.

Chapter 3 describes the steps districts and schools need to take to set up a professional development program that is differentiated and job embedded.

Chapters 4 through 6 each illustrate the implementation of one step of the "I Do, We Do, You Do" model. These chapters present the meat of differentiation in practice.

Chapter 7 expands on the roles that teacher leaders can assume in professional development. In addition to providing the coaching that is fundamental to "I Do, We Do, You Do," teacher leaders can specifically support new teachers by becoming mentors and can guide colleague-to-colleague learning by facilitating the work of collaborative teams.

Chapter 8 focuses on the creative use of time within a teacher's workday to allow participation in targeted professional development with minimal time away from students. This chapter describes a variety of successful professional development structures.

Chapter 9 considers the principles that guide administrators and the strategies that will help them as they support the professional learning of teachers. A major focus of this chapter is the paradigm shift from top-down decision making to a collaborative model that views the building administrator as part of the learning team.

Chapter 10 shares the story of the ten-year professional learning journey of the Maine-Endwell Central School District in upstate New York. This chapter documents both the research and the step-by-step process that enabled the district to become a professional learning community. For those readers beginning the journey, this story may provide some models that can be replicated. For those who have already taken the initial steps, learning about others' successes and challenges may help to illuminate the way.

We appreciate that the conditions under which teachers learn are varied and unique, and professional learning must always be designed with this awareness. As teachers participate in a myriad of job-embedded learning opportunities, they deserve only the best efforts to make each experience value-added. We hope that this book will provide our readers with a picture of successful professional development through the process of differentiation—a process that offers a comfortable environment of collegial reflection and interdependence for adults in a professional learning community.

CHAPTER 1

The Power of Differentiation

The ultimate goal of professional development is to strengthen the practice of teachers in order to raise the achievement of students (Darling-Hammond, 1997a, 1997b). The question we still need to answer is, How? How do we expand new and veteran teacher knowledge? Every district can point to efforts to support teacher learning. Nonetheless, our experience may show us that not all teachers who engaged in professional development programs learned, and not all of our students are achieving at high levels.

According to Bruce Joyce and Beverly Showers (2002), to ensure that teacher learning transfers to classroom practice, professional development must include the following four components:

1. Teachers must be provided with and understand the theory supporting a strategy.

2. Teachers must have the opportunity to watch a skillful demonstration of the strategy.

3. Teachers must be given time to practice the strategy.

4. Teachers must engage in follow-up sharing of practice and participation in peer coaching.

When professional learning is designed to include all four components, teachers engage in personal re-culturing that involves changing the way they work. With the support of collaborative teams, individuals slowly begin to do things they have never done before (Schlechty, 2005). A school should provide members of teacher teams with time to learn and practice new strategies, to watch one another practice, and then to share the results of using the strategies.

Teachers cite Joyce and Showers' fourth component of follow-up sharing and peer observations as the vital step in their ability to master new learning and consistently apply strategies that increase student achievement in their classrooms. People who work in communities are required to make commitments and trust others. For both veteran and new teachers, making a commitment to a trusted colleague can be much more effective than simply making a commitment to oneself. Individuals work together for the express purpose of making their school a place where all children learn. Being a part of a community of learners offers countless opportunities to listen and respond to differing points of view, apply creative solutions, and include more people in decision making.

The National Staff Development Council (NSDC) advises that professional learning must include continuous conversations, it must be meaningful to a teacher's work, and there must be methods to evaluate progress (Hord & Sommers, 2008). Peer coaching provides the impetus to keep the conversations going, collaborative teaming brings meaning and validation to daily work, and guided data collection and analysis within the team tracks progress and focuses thinking on student learning.

Differentiation makes it possible to include all the components necessary for successful teacher learning and becomes the foundation, the structural support, indeed the blueprint, of any professional development experience.

A Differentiation Mindset

To begin to think about differentiating professional development, it is helpful to consider the components of differentiated instruction for student learners. The work of educator and researcher Carol Ann Tomlinson provides an excellent vision for teachers, leaders, and professional development specialists. In *How to Differentiate Instruction in Mixed-Ability Classrooms* (2001), Tomlinson explains,

> In a differentiated classroom, the teacher proactively plans and carries out varied approaches to content, process, and product in anticipation of and response to student differences in readiness, interest, and learning needs. (p. 7)

It is precisely these components of readiness, interest, motivation, and learning styles, in combination with content and situation, that professional development specialists must attend to when providing learning for teachers. If one believes that differentiation is valuable for student learners, then why wouldn't differentiation be valuable for adult learners as well?

Rick Wormeli (2007, p. 7) has observed that "differentiation is foremost a professional and responsive mind-set." In other words, attending to differentiation puts the focus on what students are learning, rather than on what is being taught. Team collaboration within a professional learning community (PLC) helps a district to develop this differentiation mindset. Wormeli suggests beginning with a questioning process. Although the questions he lists are intended to help teachers start thinking about differentiation for their students, professional developers might reflect upon similar questions as they engage in planning for teacher learning:

+ Are we ready to teach using whatever methods necessary for teachers to learn?

+ "Do we have the courage to do what works, not do what is the easiest?" (2007, p. 8)

+ Can we adapt our instructional methods to match the strengths and needs of every teacher learner?

+ Do we possess a variety of instructional practices, or do we rely on one or two tried-and-true methods?

+ Do we arrange the setting to encourage learning or to be functional for us as leaders?

+ Do we keep up to date on the latest research on learning?

+ Do we persistently reflect and debrief on our professional development experiences to explore ways to improve?

+ Do we invite teacher feedback on the ability to learn in the learning environment provided?

Districts must realize that professional development requires different processes at different times, based on learners' knowledge, background, skills, and expectations. While it is nearly impossible to meet everyone's needs, all teachers deserve to learn something they can apply in their specific teaching situations. With this in mind, professional development is designed with a focus on what teachers already know as well as what they want to know. Implementing a variety of professional development opportunities ensures differentiation to help teachers connect theories, routines, and observations with the problems they face in their own classrooms.

Differentiation and Collaborative Learning

Collective learning is one of the priorities of a PLC. There are many ways to encourage teacher collaboration, and professional development can be delivered through a variety of venues. Often new learning begins in a workshop format with grade-level or departmental teams. During these sessions, team members identify what they need to learn to help more students succeed. After the theories and research have been presented, teachers collaborate to create higher-order student tasks and common assessments. Facilitators guide teams in their thinking and problem-solving activities and become keen observers of the work. Lead learners model their use of strategies and coach peers in acquiring new skills. Professional learning continues when two or more teachers develop instructional plans for their students. Co-learners visit one another's classrooms during peer observations to watch teaching methods and to interact with students. Two teachers or teams of teachers meet to reflect on student work and to identify areas for improvement and interventions to implement. At regular intervals, entire staffs come together to share the results of their work and make certain that everyone is going in the same direction with specific initiatives. In short, collaborative, differentiated, job-embedded learning focuses on:

✦ Targeting the learning

✦ Varying formats for the learning

- ✦ Coaching for the learning

- ✦ Sharing the learning

- ✦ Celebrating progress

This approach is the key to success.

One Learning Experience, Two Learners

As we will discuss in chapter 2, adult learners have certain basic needs. But those needs will manifest themselves in a variety of ways during a learning situation. Leaders of professional development have to consider the *who* as well as the *what* when they are teaching. They must realize and plan for the different ways that teacher learners may be affected by the manner in which information is presented.

Let's look at an example of the power of differentiation. One professional development challenge that districts across the country face is providing a formal mentoring program for newly hired teachers. Many states, including New York, now require teachers to receive one year of formal mentoring before they can be certified. The New York districts in which we worked provide a three-year induction program with two components. The first component is a full year of mentoring for those teachers who need to fulfill that requirement for certification. The second component, designed by the district's professional development team and induction committee, is job-embedded professional development for all newly hired teachers. This means that for three years, new teachers are acculturated into a district, not simply mentored.

When districts begin to plan such programs, they undoubtedly find that their newly hired teachers have varying backgrounds. A few teachers are beginning their very first teaching job, some have had three or four years of experience in another district or another state, some may be switching from successful careers in other fields, and some may be returning to the district after having taken time away to raise a family. Surely this diverse group will present a variety of needs, interests, life experiences, fears, levels of motivation, self-concepts, and learning styles.

As districts reflect on ways to support their newly hired teachers, they quickly realize the importance of adult learning. While all teachers will sit at the learning table, the end results will not be the same for every participant. Some of these teachers will come to the table prepared to partake fully of all the offerings and will be capable of developing the patience, putting in the necessary practice, and accepting the guidance needed to bring the information to the classroom. Some will come because they feel little or no choice. Some will come feeling like they already know the information and are wasting precious time. Some will come anxious to try every new idea during the first week of school. Some will come feeling inadequate and overwhelmed by all they are expected to know. On the first day of new-teacher orientation, it is often easy to spot the "pioneers" (those who are risk takers, eager to innovate), the "settlers" (those who will follow the pioneers once they know it is safe), and the "outlaws" (those who are rebels, resistant to change). The district must be thoughtful and very focused to temper the enthusiastic pioneers, validate and encourage the settlers, and be firm with the outlaws. (We are indebted to William Rauhauser for this metaphor.)

An important part of any professional development program for new teachers is examining the role of literacy in student learning. To see how teachers' learning experiences may be filtered through their individual needs, let's imagine that during a whole-group presentation on literacy strategies, the teacher trainer asks the teachers to independently read a short selection about the internal combustion engine and its parts. The teachers are asked to use sticky notes to record the places in the text where they are confused, where they are surprised, or where they disagree with the information. They are then to record any strategies they apply to maintain their reading comprehension. This accomplished, teachers will share their sticky notes with the whole group to discover similarities and differences in the strategies used. Making their personal approaches visible should help these new teachers become more aware of the types of reading strategies good readers employ.

Ana is a first-year teacher in her early twenties. She teaches music to grades 3–5 and is enthusiastic and optimistic about her first year.

Scott is a fifteen-year veteran who teaches language arts to tenth-grade students. He has just moved to the district from a neighboring one and is familiar with many of his new colleagues. Both teachers come to the session with the same needs: to be validated, to make a contribution to the group, to feel empowered, to understand the purpose of the learning experience, and to be challenged. But the way these two teachers perceive this learning experience turns out to be dramatically different! Each looks at the world based on a combination of life experiences, family background and culture, and previous educational experiences. Each has an expectation or a vision of professional development.

Ana, having little experience with engines of any kind, immediately feels overwhelmed by the subject matter. Being a part of the "millennial generation," she is surprised by the session's initial focus on independence and individual ideas as opposed to collaboration and "we" thinking to solve problems. The members of Generation Y, or *millennials*, are those people born from 1977 to 1986 (Wong & Wong, 2007). According to Wong and Wong, Generation Y new teachers are "receptive to working in teams, and they are good at it. They do not blink at the mention of blogging, 'Googling,' or using Wikipedia. Indeed, learning communities are their forte." With this mindset, Ana is much more comfortable when she is presented with a shared reading experience in which she initially has a partner or a small group of partners with whom to read complicated material. She has little experience with being given a problem, asked to come up with an individual solution, and then invited to present her ideas to a group. Millennials appreciate the opportunity to work collectively at the beginning of the process as opposed to later in the process. Ana is apprehensive about her ability to share her strategies or make any valid contribution to the group and begins to disengage.

Scott, on the other hand, quickly engages in the assignment. As opposed to his colleague Ana, Scott likes to work independently first and then share later in the learning process. He is able to rely on his life experiences and ample teaching knowledge of literacy. Scott spends most weekends working on his own car and those of his family and friends. He is an avid NASCAR fan and reads many car magazines. His prior knowledge allows him to comfortably work independently on this task before engaging in a dialogue with his colleagues. Scott is secure in his knowledge of engines as well as his ability to comprehend this type of text. Being a member of Generation X (born from 1965 to 1976) (Wong & Wong, 2007), he is a confident "I" thinker and feels relaxed as he shares his strategies and contributes to the discussion with this group of colleagues.

This learning exercise leaves one teacher feeling overwhelmed, inadequate, and apprehensive and the other feeling highly affirmed and validated. The way these teachers will approach future new learning has definitely been influenced by this experience. It is evident that the emotions connected with a situation and the ways in which a person interprets the situation will affect the kind of action the person will take (Burns, 1995). If this sort of experience continues, Ana may begin to view professional development as ineffectual drudgery.

Research has helped us transform our classrooms from places of "don't talk, keep your eyes on your own paper, and work independently" to arenas of social activity. Students are encouraged to talk with partners; to share ideas, questions, and solutions; and to learn from everyone in the room. Similarly, we know that adult learners benefit from collaborative work. However, as we have seen with Ana and Scott, professional development leaders must be sure of the timing for collaboration. A differentiated version of the same session on literacy strategies might have the participants begin by taking a few minutes to independently make lists of some of the reading strategies they use when confronted with complex reading or reading for which they have little or no prior knowledge. To ensure participant success and begin to build the risk-free environment hoped for in professional development sessions, the leader should be certain that every teacher in the room will have a few known strategies to list. (This certainly should be the case when working with teachers.) With the lists in hand, teachers may then pair up with partners to read and mark the text together, noting strategies that seem to be effective with this text. Now the activity's focus becomes a collaborative process, thus easing frustrations and feelings of failure for individuals. Ana, the first-year teacher, has a few ideas for her list and moves easily into the partner interaction, a situation in which she feels more confident. Scott, the more experienced "I" thinker, has time to apply his prior knowledge and is more open to listening to others after he composes a long list. Once the teachers have read and marked the text, the leader creates a chart of reading strategies the participants have used. Now all teachers have a beginning list of the things that good readers do when confronted with complex text. They have a place to begin teaching students. All participants have had the opportunity to succeed and to believe in their ability to learn. Feelings of professionalism are elevated, and value is added through the differentiated, risk-free environment.

With differentiated learning, teacher experiences are motivating and exhilarating, enhancing a sense of community and professional well-being.

A Formula for Success

As professional learning communities engage in dynamic team learning through a variety of formats, differentiation will be the spark that ignites the engine, providing the power for teacher and student success. Consider the enthusiastic comments of four teachers, each with a different learning style, whose district supported both collaborative work and differentiated professional development:

✦ An understanding learner: "The time to share lesson application and action research, particularly cross-district and cross–grade level, is very beneficial as we build bridges K–12. I'm so curious to know what others are doing, and the opportunity to share my own creativity validates me and my work."

✦ A self-expressive learner: "I appreciate the leadership provided to my team as we develop common assessments in an effort to identify struggling students. Using the strengths of each individual, our team is able to clarify and think creatively while setting attainable goals collaboratively."

◆ A mastery learner: "I need time to practice and get feedback. I welcome this day-to-day coaching as a way of realizing just how important my work with students really is. More and more of my students are making gains, and I'm feeling more and more capable."

◆ An interpersonal learner: "Being a first-year teacher, I was apprehensive about professional learning experiences that would ask for my opinions. It has been comforting to have a confidential mentor relationship. This has been a tremendous stress-buster as I engage in professional learning with veteran staff. The teaming concept has helped me feel welcome and has allowed me to build relationships with my grade-level colleagues while learning new skills along the way."

In the chapters that follow, we offer a professional development process that will provide differentiated support to enhance each teacher's instructional toolkit.

CHAPTER 2

Adult Learning Theory and a Three-Step Model for Differentiated Professional Development

It would be difficult to practice adult differentiated learning without first examining theories of both adult learning and children's learning. *Pedagogy*, often used as a synonym for teaching, is the art and science of educating children. In its narrowest sense, pedagogy refers to a model in which the teacher directs the learning by making decisions about what will be learned, how it will be learned, and when it will be learned. However, there are many different theories of pedagogy. John Dewey, for example, believed that formal education for children should be based on a learner-focused philosophy, with students learning through activities with guidance from teachers. He believed that learning was life itself, not just a preparation for life (Conner, 1997–2004).

Conditions for Children's Learning

In 2002, Brian Cambourne outlined eight conditions that must be present in classrooms if learning is to take place for children. Don Holdaway (2000) held similar theories about children's learning. Cambourne and Holdaway believed that personal interactions within a rich environment capitalized on the social nature of learning. Table 2.1 (page 18) summarizes their theories.

Table 2.1: Conditions to Promote Children's Learning

Brian Cambourne	Don Holdaway
Immersion. Children work in an environment rich in the expected learning.	**Demonstration.** Learners are immersed in environments leading to their engagement in approximating what they have observed.
Demonstration. Children are given opportunities to observe many models.	**Participation.** Learners choose which demonstrations to approximate, and the teacher (formally or informally) responds to the approximation on the spot.
Expectation. Children are given the message "You can learn."	**Role playing or practice.** The emphasis is on self-correcting to support the development of the learning.
Responsibility. Children choose what to explore and try after demonstrations.	**Performance.** The goal is to receive group acknowledgment, not to be judged better than the others.
Approximation. Children are free to make attempts as they move closer to conventions.	
Employment or use. Children have opportunities to use and practice what is being taught alone and with others.	
Response. Children receive formal and informal feedback.	
Engagement. Children actively participate in learning activities.	

Malcolm Knowles and Adult Learning Theory

In 1973, in an attempt to formulate a comprehensive adult learning theory, Malcolm Knowles published the book *The Adult Learner: A Neglected Species.* In it he said that adults as well as children require certain conditions to learn:

+ **Purpose.** Letting learners know why something will be important to them

+ **Demonstration.** Showing learners how to direct themselves through the information they are expected to learn

+ **Connection.** Relating the topic to the learner's prior experiences

+ **Motivation.** Providing purpose and satisfying needs as incentives for the learning

+ **Assistance.** Helping learners to overcome inhibitions, unproductive behaviors, and negative beliefs about learning

Knowles adopted the term *andragogy*, which originated in Germany in 1833, to define and explain these conditions. While most people associate andragogy with adult learning, Knowles himself conceded that four of his five conditions apply equally to adults and children. The exception is "connection," because children have fewer life experiences and preestablished beliefs than adults. This difference between children and adults accounts for the differences in their abilities to reflect on, analyze, synthesize, and extrapolate from the information being learned.

In addition to defining the conditions for adult learning, Knowles identified the following characteristics of adult learners:

+ Adults bring a great many experiences to the learning environment.

+ Adults expect to have a high degree of influence on what they will learn and the way they will learn.

+ Adults need to be encouraged to actively participate in designing and implementing the learning program.

+ Adults need to be able to see applications for the new learning.

+ Adults expect to have a high degree of influence on how learning will be evaluated.

+ Adults expect their responses to be acted upon when they are asked for feedback on their learning progress.

Knowles' theory of andragogy emphasized that instruction for adults should focus more on the process and less on the content being taught. This is because adults need to know why they need to learn something, they need to learn experientially, they learn best when the topic is of immediate use to them, and they approach learning as a problem-solving activity (Knowles, 1973/1997, 1975). These characteristics of adult learners mean that using simulations and case studies, employing essential questions, and asking for self-evaluations are very useful strategies for leaders of professional development.

Let's look at an example of how a teacher trainer could apply the principles of andragogy to the design and implementation of training days for secondary teachers to address reading in the content areas.

1. **Adults need to be involved in the planning of the content.** Prior to the training sessions, survey all content-area teachers about the perceived literacy needs of their students.

2. **Adults are most motivated to learn things that have immediate relevance to their job.** As an entrance task to the training, ask teachers what benefits they would enjoy if all of their students were able to comprehend the assigned reading material.

3. **Adults are goal oriented and need a specific reason for learning.** Post specific goals and intended outcomes for learning at the beginning of all working sessions.

4. **Adult learning is problem centered rather than content oriented.** Instead of using a lecture format, use instruction that is task oriented. Model instructional strategies using content materials from teachers' classrooms. Have teachers practice in small groups with facilitator feedback.

5. **Adults are self-directed and need to discover things for themselves with guidance when needed.** Take into account differences in learning styles and interests, as well as previous experiences with literacy strategies. Differentiate learning with instructional strategies such as modeling, pair sharing, peer observations, role playing, jigsaw reading, read-aloud, and shared reading.

6.   **Adults need to learn experientially and be involved in the evaluation of the learning.** Plan follow-up sessions for group sharing of practice to celebrate success and address concerns. Provide individual coaching and facilitate team collaboration during the practice period.

Teacher Learning Needs

Whether teacher learning is individualized, as in a workshop format, or collaborative, as in a team inquiry effort, it presents challenges for school districts. When teachers begin to engage in job-embedded professional development, districts must be prepared to fill the *essential needs* of each individual and team.

Teacher Learning Needs

1.   Real-world, relevant goals and objectives for learning

2.   Some control over or choice of the learning experiences

3.   Learning that matches day-to-day needs

4.   Concrete modeling, coaching, and reflection

5.   Support from peers to reduce the fear of judgment while learning

6.   Time for practice and reflective feedback

7.   Small-group participation in order to share, reflect, and generalize the learning

8.   Accommodations for diversity of knowledge, interests, self-direction, and competencies

9.   Coaching and follow-up activities to help transfer learning to daily teaching (Hord, Rutherford, Huling-Austin, & Hall, 1987; Knowles, 1973/1997)

Barry Sweeny (2003, section 1) has stated that "the best tool there is for planning professional development activity to address the individual needs of people" is the Stages of Concern, a component of the Concerns-Based Adoption Model (CBAM). Originally developed by Gene Hall and Susan Loucks-Horsley (1979), CBAM has been continually researched, and it provides an excellent foundation on which to build professional growth. Sweeny (2003) explains that "the Stages of Concern [model] defines human learning and development as going through 7 stages, during which a person's focus or concern [about learning or implementing something new] shifts in rather predictable ways" (section 2). For example, in the early stages, the learner is concerned with the potential personal impact of what he or she is being asked to learn or do. The later stages "are focused on the results and impact" of the learning (Sweeny, 2003, section 2). Learners progress through learning stages at different rates, and it would be advisable for those designing professional development to be familiar with this model and to be able to recognize and accommodate the stage each learner has reached. A good source of information on this topic is *Taking Charge of Change* (Hord et al., 1987).

The Gradual Release of Responsibility Model

Teacher learning is demonstrated through changes in behavior, such as routinely implementing a specific teaching strategy in light of an analysis of data that show improvements in student performance. In his book *The Whole Story*, Brian Cambourne (1988) tells us that learning, or behavior change, happens when the learner has models, feedback, peer support, and a lot of practice. When we look at these conditions, it is clear that an important factor in learning is *social interactions with others who are more knowledgeable*. This is the starting point for David Pearson and M. C. Gallagher's gradual release of responsibility model (1983). According to this model, learners move from novice to proficient through these interactions with more knowledgeable guides. The learning progresses through three stages: teacher modeling, joint practice and collaboration, and independent application. At each stage, the participants feel a purposeful shift in their level of accountability (responsibility) for the learning. Ultimately, the learners share their new expertise with peers, and the learning continues.

"I Do, We Do, You Do": A Three-Step Model for Differentiated Professional Development

While all the learning theories that have been discussed here are valuable to consider in planning and facilitating adult learning experiences, two in particular hold the key to a model of professional development that focuses on engagement and differentiation. They are Cambourne's conditions for learning and Pearson and Gallagher's gradual release of responsibility model.

Combining six of Cambourne's conditions for learning that appeared in table 2.1 (page 18) with the three stages of the gradual release of responsibility model gives us the three steps of our model for differentiated professional development:

Step 1.   Demonstration and expectation: teacher modeling

Step 2.   Approximation and response: joint practice and collaboration

Step 3.   Responsibility and use: independent application

Based on a more informal terminology that was introduced by Douglas Fisher and Nancy Frey (2008), we call the three steps of our model "I Do, We Do, You Do." Chapters 4 through 6 will each be devoted to one step. We believe that the "I Do, We Do, You Do" structure offers the well-developed picture of differentiated professional development that has been missing for so long.

It has become clear that simply delivering information to teachers with the expectation that it will be useful to all and that everyone will implement it does not work. Joyce and Showers (2002) have offered remarkable research concerning teachers' transfer of new knowledge to their practice:

✦   Five percent transfer new knowledge that was learned through presentations at a workshop.

✦   Ten percent transfer new knowledge when presentations are combined with demonstrations by leaders.

✦ Twenty percent transfer new knowledge when presentations and demonstrations are combined with opportunities to practice.

✦ Twenty-five percent transfer new knowledge when presentations, demonstrations, and opportunities for practice are combined with feedback.

✦ Ninety percent transfer new knowledge when ongoing coaching is combined with presentations, demonstrations, and opportunities for practice with feedback.

The "I Do, We Do, You Do" approach will maximize the transfer of new knowledge to practice.

CHAPTER 3

Setting Up Differentiated Job-Embedded Professional Development

We know that if all students are to learn, then all teachers must also learn on a daily basis. This requires a change in the landscape of professional development. For professional development to become ongoing learning, teachers need many opportunities within their school day to observe and reflect with their colleagues. In this way, teachers can "learn from their work rather than taking time away from their work to learn" (Hernez-Broome & Hughes, 2004, p. 27). Moreover, professional development should not be designed to meet short-term goals. Its purpose is to enable teachers and administrators to find the root causes for challenges and to devise long-term solutions.

First and foremost, a district or school must commit to moving adult learning forward through job-embedded professional development. Adopting the three-step model introduced in chapter 2 will then allow the differentiation of the delivery of learning to teachers. Districts and schools can implement the "I Do, We Do, You Do" model to support each data-driven initiative and target.

In order to lay the groundwork for the kind of differentiated job-embedded professional development we describe in this book, districts and schools need to determine *what* the targets are, *how* the professional development will be delivered, and *who* will introduce and support the learning. Then they must establish the optimal conditions for both teacher leaders and teacher learners. All this can be accomplished through the following steps:

1. Collect data

2. Determine initiatives and targets based on data analysis

3. Choose formats for delivering professional development

4. Encourage and select leaders/trainers/facilitators/coaches

5. Provide time and sustained training for leaders/trainers/facilitators/coaches

6. Build positive relationships and learning environment

7. Motivate adult learners and remove barriers to learning

8. Implement the "I Do, We Do, You Do" model to differentiate and sustain learning from the introduction to the embedding of concepts

1. Collect Data

Districts have many options when they begin to collect data and discover what needs to be included in their professional development plans. Administrators and professional development teams may decide to look at the literacy data in all schools. They may decide to look at the numeracy data, the social studies data, and the science data as well. Data are collected from such sources as yearly state assessments and common assessments created by school content-area departments or grade levels. Trends and patterns of student achievement are recorded, and these data are then distributed to the various PLC school teams within the district. Meanwhile, these individual teams collect any additional school data they may have, such as unit test results; student writing samples; teacher checklists and anecdotal records; and student journals, portfolios, and projects. At this point, teams begin to work with all the collected data to make informed decisions as to *what* the data are showing, enabling districts to identify possible initiatives and to establish specific targets within those district initiatives for each school, grade level, department, or content area. To illustrate, if numeracy becomes one of the district initiatives, problem solving might become the target within the numeracy initiative for all elementary schools.

2. Determine Initiatives and Targets Based on Data Analysis

As school teams begin their collaborative work with the data from each grade level, they may identify systemic gaps that require intervention through districtwide professional development. Let's say that the students at all elementary grade levels are found to be weak in math problem solving. Or perhaps data show that reading comprehension at the middle school level is weak. Analysis of the collected data will point the way to district initiatives and team targets. Whatever the weak area, teacher leaders, administrators, and/or the professional development team need to determine whether the concern is a gap in curriculum alignment or a gap in instructional delivery. Is this area one in which teachers need additional support? If so, it is the role of professional development to address these instructional gaps. Is the need at one grade level? In one school? Districtwide? What are the depth and the breadth of the need? The answers to these questions will drive an action plan for what needs to be targeted with professional development.

Student achievement data from state, district, and school assessments should be used to determine accurate professional development targets. Whenever possible, teachers must be provided with item analyses of these assessments so that teams can discuss the *implications* of the data rather than simply count the numbers of right and wrong answers for each test item. School- or district-constructed common assessments should include formative as well as summative assessments scored by a common rubric that will allow comparative data to be generated.

To effectively analyze data, we suggest that collaborative teams identify those items or tasks on which students have achieved above the ninetieth percentile or below the seventy-fifth percentile. The teams should then look at each individual test item or task and ask the following questions:

+ What are student strengths, as exhibited by the above-90 percent items? In other words, what are students doing well?

+ What do we want to be sure to celebrate and sustain?

+ What is being tested in the items where our students scored below 75 percent?

+ Are there classes where students scored much higher?

+ If yes, can those teachers pinpoint why? Are there specific strategies that all teachers can share?

+ Do we see a gap in our curriculum? Is there something that we are not teaching?

+ Is there a skill or concept that our students are missing across the board?

+ In summary, what are our strengths and where are our gaps?

The data should then be studied by vertical (cross-grade-level) teams to identify schoolwide patterns or districtwide trends so as to further specify realistic targets for each team. The goal of data analysis is to pinpoint district initiatives and team targets in order to raise the achievement of every student.

3. Choose Formats for Delivering Professional Development

Once the target of the professional development—the *what*—has been determined, the next step is to decide on the *how*—the formats for the delivery of the three-step model. For example, what will be the format for delivering the initial learning for all of the adult learners involved? This question is typically dealt with when planning the demonstrations to be used during the "I Do" stage. How long will we need? Can the initial instruction be addressed through team meetings? Would the roll-through format be applicable? Do we need to devote one of our conference days to the topic? Chapters 4 through 8 will provide in-depth examples of formats such as workshops, collaborative activities, coaching, action research in classrooms, rollthroughs, work with consultants, and reflection experiences.

4. Encourage and Select Leaders/Trainers/ Facilitators/Coaches

Once the formats have been chosen, professional development planners must determine *who* will introduce the learning in the "I Do" stage and who will support it during the "We Do" and "You Do" stages. One of the defining characteristics of differentiated job-embedded professional development is tapping or developing the internal expertise of school or district teacher leaders and having them perform these functions.

Eaker, DuFour, and DuFour (2002) point out that "in professional learning communities, administrators are viewed as leaders of leaders. Teachers are viewed as transformational leaders" (p. 22). By this, they mean that teacher leaders will make things happen. They are the closest to the action; they have the ability to move a learning community forward by affecting their colleagues in the workplace every day.

We use the term *teacher leaders* to describe all teachers who have a leadership role outside of their role with students. They are master teachers with established expertise in one or more content areas.

In this book we refer to a variety of teacher leadership roles. Let's take a moment to define and clarify these roles as well as to understand the overlap between them. Especially in smaller districts, one teacher leader may fill many roles. Larger districts may be able to afford to support expanded capacity. For example, in a small district there may be one lead teacher for each content area, while in larger districts there may be content-area lead teachers in each school. In smaller districts there may be one districtwide mentor, while in larger districts each school may have its own full-time mentor. There may be instances in which a teacher leader trains his or her colleagues on one topic and occupies the learner role in another context. Just as professional development should be differentiated to meet the needs of individual learners, the roles of teacher leaders must be differentiated to meet the needs of each PLC.

Teacher leaders can function as teacher trainers, facilitators, team leaders, lead teachers, instructional support teachers, literacy specialists, coaches, and mentors.

Teacher trainers are the professional developers responsible for bringing new learning to other teachers; they deliver the "I Do" part of the model. Sometimes training expertise already exists within the current faculty; at other times a school or district might bring in an outside consultant to train the trainers. Ideally, teacher trainers also actively participate in the "We Do" and "You Do" aspects of our model, but this is not mandatory.

Facilitators organize and focus discussions in small- or large-group settings. They do not introduce new learning but rather support the initial work of the teacher trainers by moving their group forward in the execution of a task such as curriculum writing. Facilitators might lead book talks or professional development follow-up discussions. *Team leaders* for grade-level, departmental, or interdisciplinary team meetings are examples of facilitators. Facilitators can assume a "We Do" role and/or support the "You Do" process.

Lead teachers represent specific content areas. They do not have the administrative duties of the traditional department chairperson but have the recognized expertise to be the district's or school's "go to" person for their content area. Lead teachers facilitate curriculum alignment work and might serve as teacher trainers for their subject areas.

Instructional support teachers and *literacy specialists* provide academic support for students and professional development for colleagues. Literacy specialists support students and teachers in reading, writing, listening, and speaking, while a district may deploy instructional support teachers to boost other content areas, such as numeracy.

Coaches are those teacher leaders closest to the action. They work with small groups or individual teachers to embed the new learning. As do athletic coaches, they differentiate for each teacher learner. Coaches may model strategies, co-teach, plan collaboratively, provide feedback, and arrange peer observations to support the teacher's action research. In short, they do whatever it takes to help each teacher transfer the learning to the classroom. Coaching is a prevalent source of support in the "We Do" and "You Do" stages.

Mentors support new teachers. Mentors combine all of the other teacher leader roles in their interactions with new teachers. That is to say, *all mentors are coaches*, but not all coaches are mentors. *All mentors are facilitators*, but not all facilitators are mentors. The mentoring role is all-encompassing. As mentors differentiate to meet the needs of each mentee, their activities involve all three stages of "I Do, We Do, You Do."

Table 3.1 (page 32) highlights the varying forms of teacher leadership that are discussed in more detail throughout the book. The key point to keep in mind, however, is that the name of the role is not as important as the function of the role in a differentiated model of professional development. The thrust of this book is to show how the professional development in each PLC can be structured to meet the needs of each adult learner. To reach this goal, a district or school taps the expertise of its faculty, establishing a cadre of teacher leaders who will be able to support and sustain professional learning over time.

When planning professional development, districts and schools should evaluate their in-house capacity to address their own needs. Perhaps their math lead teachers have recently attended a workshop series on problem solving. Do they now have the information and skills to train other teachers? Or would the instructional support teachers be able to research and prepare the needed information? To support listening skills, might the literacy specialists or English language arts lead teachers be appropriate trainers?

Table 3.1: Professional Development Leadership Roles

Role	Function	Focus	Who Performs
Teacher trainer	Prepares and presents workshops on specific district initiatives	"I Do"	District and school staff or outside consultants
Facilitator	Organizes and facilitates meetings and workshops in a group setting	"We Do"	District and school staff
Team leader	Facilitates specific team meetings	"We Do"	School staff
Lead teacher	Facilitates content-area meetings	"We Do"	District or school staff
Instructional support teacher or literacy specialist	Provides professional development to colleagues in a specific content area	"I Do, We Do, You Do"	District or school staff
Coach	Provides one-to-one differentiated support in the classroom setting	"I Do, We Do, You Do"	Mentor, instructional support teacher, literacy specialist, district or school staff
Mentor	Supports new teachers	"I Do, We Do, You Do"	District- or school-based mentor

Of course, a district can still bring in the occasional outside presenter for the purpose of starting conversations or introducing the staff to the research that underlies district initiatives. But these one-shot sessions have the most impact when they are followed up in PLC meetings, action research pairs, and study groups.

In general, it is good to heed Mike Schmoker's reminder that "the experts are among us" (2006, p. 114). The key is to harness the power of colleague-to-colleague support to enhance a school's or district's mission, vision, values, and goals. To this end, schools must encourage teachers to lead and put them into positions to do so.

How are teacher leaders compensated for taking on their additional responsibilities, and how does one find the time to serve as a teacher leader? In many cases, a negotiated stipend may be available. In others, substitute teachers may be provided to allow for planning time. For day-to-day coaching, rather than removing the classroom teachers from their students, it is preferable to arrange for literacy specialists, special educators, instructional support teachers, or others to provide push-in classroom support. There are other leadership positions that do not require extensive release time from the classroom. Roles such as lead teacher or team leader might be more suited to classroom teachers' schedules.

5. Provide Time and Sustained Training for Leaders/Trainers/Facilitators/Coaches

Teacher leaders must be provided with the time and resources they need for their own professional learning. In-depth training will augment their expertise in the knowledge base necessary to support district initiatives. By attending conferences on the targeted topic, working with outside consultants, engaging in book studies, or participating in professional workshops that include collaborative dialogue and reflection, these teacher leaders develop into peer coaches, the "go to" building experts who are available to answer questions and provide support daily. This colleague-to-colleague support allows adult learning to be continuous and differentiated.

Once again, it is important to seek training opportunities for teacher leaders that will require minimal time away from students. If funding is available, the leaders' training might take place after school hours or during vacation time. In some cases, current teacher leaders might serve as the trainers for other colleagues if there is a need to expand the cadre of teacher trainers.

A teacher trainer must also become an expert in the art of differentiation, allowing teacher learning to be transferred to each school's diverse classrooms. As opposed to buying the one-size-fits-all T-shirt, differentiating professional development is more like buying the baseball cap with the adjustable strap. All the teachers may need and even desire the same cap but need the adjusting strap to ensure a proper fit. Effective trainers must have the skills to manage groups, validate prior knowledge, and identify individual strengths and needs. As they listen to and observe the participants, they determine the differentiation that will be necessary for each teacher to accept new ideas, practice new methods, participate in coaching experiences, and independently use new practices with students. Teachers who are peer coaches must be able to keep making adjustments along the learning journey in terms of time, amount of information provided, format for instruction, and individualized coaching language. They must be able to create multiple pathways to accommodate the differences in learners' abilities, interests, and needs.

By funding professional development for their teacher leaders and purchasing professional books and support materials, districts position these leaders for success in their role as teachers teaching teachers.

6. Build Positive Relationships and Learning Environments

Enjoying positive feelings in a learning situation increases the likelihood of success. Thus districts must attend to developing good relationships between those giving and those receiving information and must also carefully consider the environment in which the learning is to take place (Given, 2002; Tomlinson, 2003; Wolfe, 2001). These two elements—positive relationships and environments—will provide districts with the foundation for the differentiation that is instrumental in implementing job-embedded learning.

In her book *Leadership and the New Science* (2006), Margaret Wheatley explores the ideas of relationships and organizational power.

She concludes that it is not the tasks, functions, roles, or positions of people that give organizations power. Rather, she says, "power in organizations is the capacity generated by relationships" (p. 39).

Roland Barth (2006) tells educators that to grow learning communities, they must become collegial and learn to "play together." He lists the following conditions as evidence of collegiality:

+ Educators talking with one another about practice.

+ Educators sharing their craft knowledge.

+ Educators observing one another while they are engaged in practice.

+ Educators rooting for one another's success. (p. 10)

Barth concludes that without these collegial relationships, "no meaningful improvement—no staff or curriculum development, no teacher leadership, no student appraisal, no team teaching, no parent involvement, and no sustained change—is possible" (p. 13).

Tomlinson (2003) notes that positive affect and a positive learning environment are the catalysts for effective differentiation. The following questions can help district administrators, teacher trainers, and professional development facilitators build positive relationships and a positive learning environment for differentiated professional development:

+ Will participation be voluntary?

+ Will the expectations for participants be explicit and attainable?

+ Will participants provide input to facilitators regarding content needs prior to the work?

+ Will participants be offered a variety of opportunities to demonstrate their learning?

+ Will participants have some choice in goal setting and practice methods?

+ Will participants be offered the necessary resources to enable transfer of new knowledge to daily practice?

+ Will participation be embedded within the workday?

+ Will participants collaborate and share responsibilities?

+ Will there be a balance between serious work and the celebration of success?

A district that can answer yes to these questions is well on its way to providing the differentiation necessary for successful learning.

The first question requires further discussion, however. Voluntary participation is expected to produce better learning that will most likely transfer to embedded practice in classrooms. Schools should make every attempt to offer choice and to sustain a volunteering atmosphere. However, some professional development falls into the compulsory category by virtue of being legally mandated or just plain necessary for the benefit of students. When this becomes the case, a professional developer has an even greater responsibility to tend to the remaining conditions identified in the list. Teachers can be given choices regarding the structure of the learning, the ways to adapt the learning, the timelines for implementation of the learning, the types of support they need or prefer, and the colleagues with whom they would like to work for practice. Ultimately, it is the goal of the professional developer to build individual relationships with the participants. Simply put, when differentiation is applied to a learning situation, even the most unwilling participants are able to feel freedom of choice, and minds can begin to open.

7. Motivate Adult Learners and Remove Barriers to Learning

When planning and engaging in adult learning situations, leaders think about how they can ensure active participation that will result in the intended learning. They might ask themselves, What can I do to help my learners get started? What can I do to encourage more effort on their part? How can I create a relevant and meaningful learning environment? These questions relate to motivation, and we know that when there is no motivation to learn, there is no learning (Walberg and Uguroglu, 1979). The cliché "You can lead a horse to water, but you cannot make it drink" is easily appreciated in the world of education. Motivation is a personal internal process that moves one to accomplish something or to satisfy a need. The differences we find in the performance of learners of equal ability are mainly due to motivation (Burns, 2002).

According to Stephen Lieb (1991, section 2), there are at least six factors that motivate adults to learn: "social relationships, external expectations, social welfare, personal advancement, escape/stimulation, and cognitive interest." Success is without a doubt a further, vital motivating force for educators. When districts build in success for all participants, the motivation quotient soars. Instead of applying one band-aid after another to the same wound, districts can empower teachers to operate as a learning community of professionals, using data to inform decisions and continuously collaborating to find long-term solutions that will enable all students and teachers to achieve their learning potential.

Professional development has a better chance of having a positive impact on student learning when the majority of the school community has a voice in its conception, design, timing, and content. When teachers actively participate in determining what the targets will be, as discussed in steps 1 and 2, they understand the purpose behind the professional development initiatives and will support their implementation. However, positive results can still be achieved without having everyone on board as professional development is initiated. To build in success, districts might begin by enlisting the pioneers who are ready and eager to give the new learning a try. The settlers will board the train when colleagues spread the word and demonstrate the progress they have made with the new ideas. Sometimes leaders must start to move a large group one person at a time. The sharing in learning communities does more to spark interest in change than any bidding of administrators.

Coupled with the need to motivate teachers is the need to remove any barriers that prevent them from participating in learning activities. As do all adults, teachers have a variety of responsibilities that must be balanced with their ongoing learning. The natural tendency is to resist adding more. How often do we hear these objections? "I don't have time this month." "I'm not interested in another new fad!" "My schedule doesn't allow me to take part in this right now." "These team meetings create too much paperwork and follow-up stuff for me!" "I'm trying to have a life, you know." "I have child-care issues." "I've been teaching for twenty years, and my kids do just fine. Are you trying to tell me that what I've been doing all along is wrong?"

We continue to search out answers. The best way to motivate adults is to enhance their reasons for participating in professional development and to make the learning as relevant and convenient as we can. When teachers recognize the relationship between their learning and increased student achievement, they are more willing to participate (and less likely to be outlaws).

Let's look at an example of guiding teachers in this direction. In a meeting with her math teachers, Ms. Ogawa, a middle school principal, asks, "What would be the advantages if your students were better equipped to comprehend word problems?"

Ellen responds, "Being able to cover more content in less time and at a deeper level of understanding would be a clear advantage."

Mike offers, "And being able to incorporate a common literacy language with other content-area teachers would strengthen our entire program and make our interdisciplinary work more connected for students."

Having realized some possibilities, the teachers are now more receptive when Ms. Ogawa tells them that reading in the content areas would be the perfect series of learning sessions for them to attend. Anticipating potential barriers to their motivation, she assures them,

"I will work with the presenters to make sure that only math teachers will be involved; we won't be asking you to extrapolate from examples in other content areas and tweak them for math." She also arranges for the learning sessions to take place for two hours during the day so that the teachers will have to leave their classrooms only briefly, not for days at a time.

When the teachers arrive at the first session, Ms. Fernandez, the trainer, begins by asking them, "What do you need to get out this session?"

Ellen replies, "I need to know how reading-in-the-content-area strategies will allow me to cover more material rather than being something extra that I need to pile onto everything else I have to cover."

"Great," Ms. Fernandez responds, "then let's focus today on key math vocabulary that is common in many math word problems."

Interest in the subject (math word problems), coupled with enlightened self-interest (what I'll get from better student performance), becomes a tremendous motivator for learning. When the math teachers see how these learning sessions will benefit them pragmatically, they are motivated to attend, to perform well, and finally to transfer their new knowledge to their daily practice. Cognitive coaching and purposeful feedback sustain the benefits of the learning and lead to requests from teachers for additional learning.

Applying differentiation to professional development projects is a further way to eliminate motivational barriers. Responding to adults' readiness, interest, and learning styles by varying instructional strategies, pacing, the complexity of the tasks, and the level of facilitator support enables all adult learners to succeed. In addition, modeling the differentiation of content, process, and product in the delivery of professional development gives participants numerous opportunities to talk with their colleagues about how differentiation works in a responsive classroom (Tomlinson, 1999).

Increase Motivation and Reduce Learning Barriers

✦ Give teachers opportunities to design the content of the learning based on personal needs and student data.

✦ Appreciate teachers' diversity and experiences.

✦ Give teachers purpose and value for their learning.

✦ Assure teachers of flexibility in grouping and pacing.

✦ Offer differentiation to address individual/team needs.

✦ Offer a choice of methods to demonstrate learning.

✦ Offer follow-up activities based on understanding and ability.

✦ Offer opportunities to engage in reflection and collaboration with fellow learners.

✦ Challenge teachers to meet high but attainable expectations.

✦ Offer opportunities for self-evaluation.

8. Implement the "I Do, We Do, You Do" Model to Differentiate and Sustain Learning From the Introduction to the Embedding of Concepts

Chapters 4 through 6 will explain in detail how the "I Do, We Do, You Do" model provides each adult learner with a differentiated job-embedded learning path that will lead to increased student achievement.

Putting It All Together

Let's take a look at how a district might set up and implement one initiative for differentiated job-embedded professional development led by teachers. Listening in on a meeting of the district professional development team will help us understand how the eight steps for setting up differentiated job-embedded professional development frame their planning. The team is made up of teachers and administrators from all schools and central office administrators.

The team facilitator is Dr. O'Donnell, the assistant superintendent for instruction. She greets the team and summarizes the work at hand. "Welcome, everyone, to this important discussion. Today's agenda is an ambitious one! We have all come prepared for a rich discussion of the conclusions from our research on the impact of literacy instruction across the content areas. We will also be reviewing our student achievement data by content area and working to finalize the professional development goals for our five-year plan. Just to recap, at our last meeting we reaffirmed our commitment to job-embedded professional development. Regardless of the professional development target, our district is committed to this model. Also, at our last meeting, William offered to be the facilitator of our discussion on the literacy research. Shall we begin?"

William, who is a high school literacy specialist, now assumes the role of facilitator. "Good morning, everyone. First off, thanks to all of you for devoting your time to the reading and research that we have done as a team over the past several months. Also, I want to recognize my colleagues on the K–12 literacy team for providing the articles and book summaries that have made it possible for this team to cover a lot of ground. Today, we are going to synthesize what we've learned to decide if we are on the right course in focusing on literacy across the content areas as the next prong of our professional development plan. I sent all of you an email requesting that you jot down some 'aha moments' from your reading and come prepared to share. Anyone want to start?"

Meghan, a sixth-grade teacher, is the first to speak. "I thought that Kelly Gallagher's *Reading Reasons* really brought home the importance of reading and its impact on student achievement across all content areas. I know that our grade 6 team could really benefit from more work on this topic."

The team members continue to discuss the research and conclude that they are on the right track.

Dr. O'Donnell acknowledges the group's efforts and moves to the next topic. "William, thank you for facilitating our discussion, and thanks, everyone, for your active participation. Let's turn now to our data. At our last meeting, we reviewed the data from all of our district teams showing that they had targeted reading and writing in the content areas as weaknesses. We asked our team members to return to their grade-level and department teams to look more closely at students' work and to pinpoint more specific targets. What do you have to report?" (**Step 1: Collect data**)

Coleta, a middle school math teacher, shares, "As we looked more closely at our data from the state math assessments and our common midterms, we discovered that our students really struggled with the word problems. It was not so much the computation as not understanding what the questions asked."

Ian, a high school science teacher, responds, "That's interesting, because we also found that many of our students' errors were based on gaps in understanding of key vocabulary words."

Amelia, a third-grade teacher, chimes in, "When we looked at data in math, word problems were an area of weakness for our kids as well, and we also have talked about vocabulary being an issue in all subject areas. It looks as if we may have a trend across the grade levels."

The discussion continues, with the resulting conclusion that the district's data and current research on the impact of literacy on achievement across the content areas converge to validate the team's plan. (**Step 2: Determine initiatives and targets based on data analysis**)

Dr. O'Donnell again expresses her appreciation. "Great work! You have all brought the results of your teams' work to the table, and we have a plan. Our next task is to determine how we will structure the professional development." (**Step 3: Choose formats for delivering professional development**)

Emiko, an elementary special educator, suggests, "The reports from all of the teams show many common elements across the content areas. As a special educator, it is great for me to make these connections for my students. Connections are important for adult learners as well. I think that this is a topic that could be presented in a large-group format."

Benjamin, a high school art teacher, has doubts. "Maybe so, but in my last district I went to so many workshops that didn't apply to art; it was a total waste of my time. I can see the commonalities here, but I need to leave a workshop with something that pertains specifically to art."

Abigail, an instructional support teacher for middle school math, responds with another suggestion. "I know what Ben means. Maybe we could start out with a type of 'keynote' that would establish the purpose for all, perhaps on an early release day. Then we could schedule follow-ups that are content-specific."

Binu, an elementary principal, builds on this idea. "I like Abigail's suggestion. Providing an initial common experience with content-specific reflection and follow-up would be a good start. Then we could further our differentiated model with additional colleague-to-colleague support in the embedding stages. Perhaps we should charge William with going back to the literacy team to get their input on how to proceed. We need to think about who will be our trainers. Our literacy team is a logical place to start."

The team members continue their discussion. They decide to follow Binu's plan and set their next agenda to include input from the literacy team.

Dr. O'Donnell exclaims, "Wow! We really accomplished a lot today! Thank you all for your time. To recap, we agreed to move forward with a professional development initiative that focuses on literacy across the content areas. We have affirmed that our analysis of student achievement and our research on best practices support this plan. We are leaning toward a combination of formats for the 'I Do' portion of our professional development. We concur that a K–12 presentation will help establish a common purpose but that we also need to have the basic tenets translated to relate to each content area. This will enhance staff buy-in.

"We are now ready for the planning step of selecting trainers. [**Step 4: Encourage and select leaders/trainers/facilitators/coaches**] William will meet with the K–12 literacy team to get their recommendations. I would also ask each building principal to reflect with his or her planning team and identify staff who might wish to serve as trainers or coaches as we move forward in this endeavor. From our past experience, we know that we are committing to a process, not an event. Our planning of each step is crucial. Slow and steady wins the race. Thanks again for a productive meeting! I'm already anxious to continue our discussion next month!"

This district has clearly been working as a professional learning community for years. Its process shows a comfort with the steps for setting up differentiated job-embedded professional development. The planning team members studied the educational research clearly establishing literacy as the key to unlocking student achievement across the content areas. Based on their reviews of their learning teams' data analyses, they decided that providing professional development on this topic would be the logical "next step" in their professional development plan. As advocates of job-embedded professional learning, the team members concluded that growing the expertise of each building's literacy specialist was a good place to start in establishing ongoing site-based professional learning. The team was facilitated by a district administrator but was made up of representatives from all buildings so that all stakeholders could take part in the planning. The agenda and planning steps were clear, and one has the impression that this type of planning is a natural part of the district's culture as a PLC.

As William returns to his K–12 literacy team to discuss potential trainers, the team members may find that they themselves possess the necessary expertise to lead the professional development. Or there may be literacy specialists or other teacher leaders who would love to step up to the plate if provided with further professional development. Another possible arrangement would be to find an outside consultant who would be the "keynote" speaker at the outset and then train in-house staff to be the follow-up facilitators and coaches. This consultant would continue to work with the cadre of in-house teacher leaders as the initiative took root. In time, in-house facilitators might develop the confidence and expertise to take over the role of teacher trainer.

The district planning team is not organizing a one-shot event; it is planning for long-term, sustained professional learning. This is a process that takes place at the inception of any initiative. Once the leaders have been selected, the team will proceed to plan steps 5 through 8, providing the resources and training necessary for the leaders to successfully implement the desired professional development.

Let's fast-forward and envision how this initiative might evolve.

Throughout the process, the literacy specialists and other trainers continue their own learning journey with group book talks and conference attendance to strengthen both their vision and purpose. While conducting the training of the content-area teachers, the literacy specialists and other teacher trainers become aware of the learning styles and needs of their learners, enabling both the teacher leaders and the participants to develop theoretical understanding together.

The participants' initial learning is enhanced when it is possible for follow-up sessions to be supported by the teacher leaders who facilitated the original professional development. By coming together to reflect on successes and struggles in implementing the literacy strategies, participants learn from their peer learners as well as from their leaders. When literacy specialists and other teacher trainers provide push-in services in classrooms, colleague-to-colleague support and individualized differentiated coaching are available. Dialogue and clarification are consistent. Follow-up and reflection become crucial steps for teams to strengthen their daily practice. As teacher communities learn together, cultures and the things that teachers do in their classrooms begin to change.

CHAPTER 4

Demonstration and Expectation: "I Do"

In the first step of the professional development process, "I Do," teacher leaders demonstrate and "do" the objective of the learning. They also set up the expectation for learner success.

Demonstration

Whether in the context of a workshop session, small-group or individual coaching, or team collaborations, demonstrations are crucial to the learning process. As more knowledgeable others describe a theory or model a process for new learners, they create a risk-free environment for learning. This showing-how step is essential for learner engagement and the future application of learning. During this step, the teacher leader assumes complete responsibility for the performance of tasks. Through a variety of demonstrations that use the thinking-aloud process, teacher trainers make the learning transparent for every learner. The use of "I" statements, such as "I think," or "I find this part interesting," or "I wonder if," invites the learner into the mind of the trainer. This helps learners to understand not only how something is done, but also how to make decisions along the way in order to complete a task (Fisher & Frey, 2008). In essence, the trainer says to participants, "Watch what I do, and listen to how I think."

Step 1 is not the time to ask learners questions or simply to give out information, but rather is a time to model cognitive (what I know) and metacognitive (how I know) processes. In order to help learners move from "this is how to do it" to "this is when to do it," teacher leaders must engage in the public problem-solving process of meta-cognition. When leaders think out loud while problem solving, perform the steps of a process, and provide the environment that leads to participant engagement, they motivate teachers to believe in personal and group success.

Leading teacher learners through the expected learning is no easy task. Language is crucial as a demonstration unfolds. "Watch how I hold the book when I read aloud." "Notice how I move among the pairs of children." "Listen to my phrasing and tone of voice as I model a student conference." "Note my body language when I join a group of children working on this project." "Pay attention to how I sequence and scaffold my questions to check for student understanding." When learners watch and listen to what "I Do," their understanding grows.

The "I Do" stage is when the teacher leader clears up misconceptions, validates and fine-tunes prior knowledge, and discovers the individual strengths and limitations of the group. At this stage, the leader begins to plan the appropriate differentiation by considering such questions as:

+ Who will need more "I Do" demonstrations?

+ Who works best alone to solve problems?

+ Who would be more successful teaming with a partner?

+ Who needs help in articulating understanding?

+ Who is motivated and why?

+ Who feels threatened by this process?

+ What can I do to alleviate fears while setting realistic expectations for every individual?

+ Have I provided enough examples, analyzed learners' challenges, approached this from different angles?

+ Have I kept my differentiation mindset?

Expectations for Learning

One way to bring a diverse group together around any expectation is to provide purpose for the learning. Helping learners direct themselves through a common experience often can provide a foundation for the process that follows. For example, taking a cue from Cambourne's research, discussed in chapter 2, the leader might ask learners to create personal learning theories—to identify the conditions that have helped them to acquire new skills: "What are the essential things that you need to be successful with learning?" To help them get started, the leader would focus on something he or she recently learned outside of a classroom setting, such as quilting, cooking, sailing, or text messaging. Then the learners would create a list of all the things they need to experience in order to become proficient at new tasks.

When leaders conduct this exercise, the item that appears most frequently on teachers' lists is watching a demonstration by someone who is more experienced. Receiving positive feedback that builds the expectation of success also appears on every list. Many other components for learning emerge, validating everyone's learning style. After comparing lists and identifying common factors, learners appreciate the *show, don't tell* approach as a necessary step for their learning. Establishing the value of and purpose for demonstrations helps to diminish the "I already know how" or the "Why do I need this?" attitude of some learners. Immersion in the activity focuses the new learning and builds social trust among the diverse teacher participants.

After the teachers create and share their personal learning theories, the leader continues the process of demonstration. Based on the discussion, participant questions, and what these teachers need to know and be able to do, the leader now decides on the most appropriate models to implement during further "I Do" demonstrations within this session as well as in the future.

A Team Experiences Step 1

In chapter 1, we mentioned the workshop format with grade-level or departmental teams as one avenue for achieving collaborative professional development. Let's look in on a middle school English language arts (ELA) team that is beginning a journey to implement literacy skills into daily content. This team is also part of the district's PLC initiative and is made up of diverse colleagues: some veterans, some newly hired teachers, and some teachers who are new to the grade level.

In response to the district's literacy initiative, Bret, the principal, has hired an outside consultant to present a two-day workshop for the team members during their summer break. Bret and the special education teachers will join the team in this Step 1 demonstration of balanced literacy. The teachers will hear definitions of terms, watch demonstrations of strategies, discuss instructional time frames and structures, and design individual action research questions to explore in their individual classrooms.

Ms. Clark, the consultant, opens the first day of training by establishing her purpose and validating the needs of the group. "I understand from your administrators that you are looking for ways to integrate more literacy learning within your ELA content curriculum. Could you go around the circle and identify one or two specific topics that you might be most interested in hearing about in the next two days?"

Teri, a four-year veteran of the team, goes first. "I feel that I have been teaching literacy, but I would like some definitions explained and perhaps modeled, like the term *balanced literacy for middle school* that we are hearing."

Sam, a first-year teacher, shares, "I don't really know what my ELA curriculum consists of yet. I'm really overwhelmed with the idea of infusing literacy strategies into my classes. I guess I need some definitions worked out also."

Val, a special education teacher who pushes in and pulls out students, describes her situation. "My job is one of supporting the teacher and the students. I'm not sure how I help the kids with literacy and ELA content all at the same time. It seems like I have to be most aware of the gaps that exist in the kids' knowledge of ELA. How do I fit into this new literacy world?"

Ms. Clark senses some resistance building as the conversation continues.

Barb, who is a twenty-year veteran of teaching but new to this team, is clearly unhappy with the whole prospect. "I'm wondering why the ELA team is being charged with this initiative. Don't we already have content to teach? We don't even have a literacy specialist on our staff. Who is going to help us after you leave in two days? What are the other content areas going to be expected to do in terms of teaching literacy?"

Carole, who is new to the grade level, has a more positive outlook. "I'll admit I'm nervous about moving from the elementary level to middle school, but I have been using this balanced literacy model with my students for several years, and I can see where, with some tweaking, it could be just as beneficial to our kids. I think we should spend some time fleshing out definitions of terms and lay out the expectations for our work."

Bret then addresses the group. "I know you have concerns, but I think once you understand the 'what,' the 'who,' the 'why,' and the 'when' of this concept, you'll be able to make some real impact with the kids. We will not just take this one first step together but will continue with more workshops and coaching with Ms. Clark throughout the year."

Ms. Clark now has a jumping-off place from which to begin Step 1 and her demonstrations. She spends the morning modeling definitions connected with the theory that will guide the year's work and then having the participants break up into dialogue pairs and discussion groups. By the end of day two, the team has been introduced to a balanced literacy framework for teaching and become acquainted with a list of strategies they will be expected to learn and use with their students. They have seen Ms. Clark model, and, to reinforce the ideas, they have also seen a video with teachers like themselves discussing terms and setting individual and team goals.

Our example ELA team members now have some focus, and they know what it is that they are going to be doing beyond this initial workshop. They have decided to have Ms. Clark—now affectionately known as "Coach"—co-teach with them for the first few months of the school year so that they can continue to see how it is possible to weave literacy into their content. Individual members of the team have started their action research by identifying which pre-reading strategies they would like to implement at the beginning of the year. "Coach" will plan and model within their classrooms to help them see how to bring their action research to life and develop the next logical steps they will need to take.

This initial workshop format has helped Ms. Clark establish a risk-free environment and observe the individual strengths of the participants.

As these team members continue to plan, co-teach, observe, and collaborate with the consultant and with one another, new teaching habits will become routine, and beliefs will solidify. This team of researchers will begin to collect data and revise their plans and their questions. They will take the initial knowledge and demonstrations back to their classrooms and reproduce them with students. While their work is still in the beginning phases, they will continue to benefit from collaboration, engaging in "This is how you do it" conversations during team meetings.

Differentiating Demonstrations

Helping teacher learners believe in new skills through demonstrations that are doable, purposeful, and differentiated is critical in Step 1. Not everyone responds to the same type of demonstration. While participants benefit from a leader's thinking aloud, some also need video presentations or opportunities to watch colleagues who are already proficient with the strategies. Peer observations often reveal aspects of a strategy that the learner did not notice in the leader's modeling. After observing colleagues, engaging in continued collaborative dialogue with team members also clarifies the thinking process for most new learners, adding additional layers of understanding.

Demonstrations during the "I Do" stage should consist of all the things a learner can see, hear, talk about, or otherwise experience as a way of learning before he or she is ready to make a first attempt. The Chinese proverb "Sometimes you must go slow to go fast" can be a guiding force for schools and districts. When the appropriate demonstration models are matched to the participants, the likelihood of teacher and student learning is greatly increased. One of the intended outcomes of showing teachers how something can be done is to enable them to become demonstrators in their own classrooms. The "I Do" step begins the progression of moving teacher learners from being receivers of knowledge to being producers of knowledge.

Let's consider an example of differentiated demonstrations for a group of intermediate elementary teachers. The teachers have decided they need assistance in preparing their students to read, analyze, and compose written responses to document-based questions. Their principal asks Tom, the school's literacy specialist for grades 3, 4, and 5, to prepare and facilitate a training to answer the teachers' needs.

To help determine the content and demonstrations he will present in the initial session, Tom sends out a short email survey to the teachers expected to attend his training:

> Colleagues:
>
> In an effort to make our time together valuable for all involved, would you please take a few minutes to complete the following survey questions and return them to me by next Monday? Thanks in advance for your interest and enthusiasm!—Tom
>
> 1. What are two things you are currently doing to prepare your students for document-based written responses?
>
> 2. What are your frustrations about teaching this type of writing? Examples: Time? Knowledge of task? Strategies?
>
> 3. Can you identify a specific aspect of this writing you would like help with?
>
> 4. Do you like to work independently or in groups while you learn?

After reading and compiling the teachers' survey responses, Tom decides that the first strategy he will demonstrate will be "marking the text." He also lays out the sequence of steps he will follow whenever he introduces a strategy:

1. Name the strategy to be learned. ("First, I will show you how readers can mark a text while reading to locate information related to the question they must answer.")

2. State the purpose of the strategy. ("It is important for your students to be able to locate the important information within the text so they have some words to use in their writing to answer the question.")

3. Explain when to use the strategy. ("When I know that I must take information from a text and combine it with my own thinking to create a written response, I read slowly, and I specifically mark the text as I read. I remember to use sticky notes or mark directly on the text.")

4. Link prior knowledge to the new strategy. ("I think about this marking like the first step toward scoring a goal in basketball. It's like dribbling, setting myself on the path that puts me in a scoring position. If I mark the text to help me identify important information, I'm on a path to be able to 'score' a correct response to the question.")

5. Demonstrate the use of the strategy. ("I'm going to show you a question and a two-paragraph text related to the question. I'll read aloud slowly and will use my highlighters to mark every sentence I read. I'll use yellow to highlight the information I think I might use to answer the question. I'll use blue to highlight the information that I think is not going to help me. I'll tell you why I'm highlighting as I read.")

6. Talk about the errors to avoid when using the strategy. ("I have to remember to reread the question as I work with my highlighter. Am I using one color more than the other?

Is there important information in every paragraph of a document? Do I understand the question well enough to be able to mark this text?")

7. Check the use of the strategy. ("Now, let me see if I have enough information to use to write an answer to the question. Yes, I can begin by saying . . .")

The day of the session, Tom follows his plan to introduce the marking strategy and model it for the whole group. After doing so, he is ready to provide different demonstration options. He asks the teachers, "Now that you've seen me go through the steps of marking the text, would you like to pair up and try it yourselves?"

Michon, a fifth-grade teacher, is hesitant. "I'm not sure I'm totally clear on this yet. I'd be interested in watching the video you mentioned that shows the sixth-grade teacher using this strategy with her students."

Adriane, who also teaches grade 5, seems relieved that Michon has brought up this possibility. "Yeah, I'd like to watch that before I try it myself."

Tom is glad to provide this option. "Sure, I'll set that up in the back of the room for anyone who's interested. Then I'll come back here to answer questions that any of the rest of you have and guide those of you who are ready to give this a try. I've got some documents here that we can use."

Some teachers from the same grade level agree to pair together to talk and try the marking strategy. A few inquire about the possibility of observing Tom model the strategy with their students in the classroom. Tom makes himself available for whatever help is needed while making sure not to set the expectation that everyone will mark a text during this meeting.

After participants have watched the video and engaged in a question/answer period, Tom provides a reflection journal prompt for the teachers. He wants to be sure that everyone has had time to process the demonstrations, clear up any confusion, and begin to internalize this initial strategy for helping their students. The responses will enable Tom to decide which teachers need more demonstrations and which ones are ready to attempt implementation of the learning in their classrooms.

Journal prompt:

Please spend the next ten minutes independently thinking and responding to the following questions in the journal I've provided:

1. What did you learn about the "marking the text" strategy that you think will help your students the most in responding to document-based questions?

2. What are your goals for implementing this learning? Decide on a timeline for your work.

3. If you need more help, what do you need?

Before the meeting ends, Tom establishes plans for follow-up work with the group to introduce additional strategies for their classrooms. The expectation is set that all teachers will eventually implement the "marking the text" strategy in their classrooms, but they will choose their own way of practicing and their own schedule for doing so. Tom knows that during the "We Do" stage—possibly with coaching, co-teaching, peer reflection on student data, and interactive journaling with students—these teachers will solidify their practice and have guidance toward the independent use of this strategy. For now, Tom's job has been to begin the process of demonstrations and start this group of teachers on their way to the next step. While a few of the team members will need to engage in several more demonstrations from a variety of colleagues, some are ready to begin the "We Do" attempts of replicating demonstrations. If districts and schools establish the same "finish line" for everyone, then there is no differentiation, and only a few teachers will find success with transferring their new learning into classroom practice.

A Foundation of Trust

The ability to learn from observing others is rooted in a trusting environment. Learning means changing. Changing means taking risks. In one of his memorable formulas, author and business consultant Tom Peters states, "The degree to which one takes risks is inversely proportional to the potential for being shot" (York-Barr, Sommers, Ghere, & Montie, 2001, p. 24). When districts offer differentiation in their professional development programs, they give teachers options based on their learning needs. This approach helps teachers feel less threatened, and possibilities for sustained growth are more likely.

To trust oneself and others means that participants must listen with open minds and observe without judgment. Professional developers must strive for their audience both to maintain awareness and to suspend personal thinking long enough to focus on the demonstration at hand. Isaacs (1999, p. 135) says, "To suspend is to change direction, to stop, step back, and see things with new eyes. This is perhaps one of the deepest challenges humans face—especially once they have staked out a position." How many teachers engage in professional development with preconceived ideas of best practice? In *Reflective Practice to Improve Schools*, Jennifer York-Barr, William A. Sommers, Gail S. Ghere, and Jo Montie (2001) state that if learners do not listen well, they will not learn well. Most listening experiences involve filtering the speaker's message to match one's own beliefs or prior knowledge. Therefore, many messages are misinterpreted or lost entirely (Carlson & Bailey, 1997; Isaacs, 1999). That is why the methods of demonstration should be chosen carefully and the foundation of trust firmly established. How can we connect with one another, as Stephen Covey (1989) suggests, through understanding, but not necessarily by agreeing? When professional development creates an environment of understanding, educators find it easier to keep negative thoughts from interfering with new thinking.

The Power of Demonstration

In *Engaging Adolescent Learners*, ReLeah Cossett Lent (2006, p. 112) observes that "the engagement of teachers has everything to do with the engagement of students." Thus, if job-embedded professional development is to have an impact on student learning, we must consider the engagement process. Engagement involves action on the part of learners. In Step 1, through "I Do" demonstrations, leaders invite questions, develop common vocabulary, propose action research, and build intellectual momentum for district initiatives.

Lent also tells us that "as teachers come to understand the power of demonstration as the infusion of knowledge and skills intertwined with the artifacts and actions of learning, they begin to rethink learning itself" (2006, p. 35). An enthusiastic response to demonstrations can propel learners into Step 2, which will offer opportunities for practice, feedback, reflection, and continued practice.

CHAPTER 5

Approximation and Response: "We Do"

Step 2: "We Do" is an explosion of activity and decision making. In the learning process, *trying it* naturally follows *watching it*. With Step 2, the gradual release of responsibility for the learning begins its steady shift. Teacher learners approximate the demonstrations of teacher leaders, guided by specific feedback and supported by collaboration.

The connective tissue between the demonstrations in Step 1 and the collaborative work of teacher and learner in Step 2 is *engagement*. According to Cambourne (1988), engagement occurs when learners are convinced that:

+ They are potential "doers" of demonstrations

+ They will further the purposes of their lives if they engage with the demonstrations

+ They can engage without fear of physical or psychological hurt if their attempts are not fully correct

Learning in Context

While teachers strive to create the optimal learning environment for students, they themselves seldom experience suitable conditions for their own learning. In *The Six Secrets of Change*, Michael Fullan speaks to the importance of embedding teachers' learning in the workday. He asserts that "learning on the job, day after day, is the work" (2008, p. 86). This "learning in context" is the thrust of the "We Do" stage.

"We Do" is the time for learners to step up to the plate and practice what they have seen in the "I Do" modeling. Participants in differentiated professional development enjoy a variety of activities through which to practice. Teachers either jump directly into modeling with students, decide to watch their coach do more modeling, or agree to co-plan and co-teach with a colleague to perfect their skills. Some will join teams to study more and engage in action research in the classroom to answer important questions that lead to yet more discovery and action. Others will seek a competent colleague with whom to gather and share data and analyze how, or if, their classroom practice is changing student accomplishments. Regardless of the differentiated road a teacher takes, if she participates in some form of coaching, she will find value in professional development, learn new roles for teaching, experience a certain level of success, contribute to the advancement of her colleagues and educational community, and most importantly, feel the joy of student achievement.

Differentiation in Step 2

Four elements are essential to Step 2: "We Do." The coaches who differentiate the "We Do" stage must remember that these four elements are not necessarily linear or time-bound but are customized for each teacher:

1. **Reflect.** Teachers reflect on the various demonstrations they have witnessed during Step 1: "I Do."

2. **Design action research.** Teachers choose the strategies they will begin to implement in their classrooms and how and when they will do so. Not every learner is required to begin with the same strategy. Instead, the teachers' action plans indicate their reasons for choosing specific strategies, the goals they intend to accomplish, the resources they will use, and the kinds of coaching they might need. The teachers make their choices based on their own readiness, interest, or learning styles, coupled with the readiness, interest, learning needs, and learning styles of their students. This results in a differentiated approach to learning for both

teachers and students. The action plans continually evolve but serve as the catalyst for the action in classrooms and the collaboration within teams.

Lent (2006, pp. 136–37) suggests an action research process:

   a.   Create a focus question to explore

   b.   Collect and organize data from your classroom activities

   c.   Analyze the data for insights related to your focus question

   d.   Construct an answer to your question and test it with your data

   e.   Decide what action you will take to address your question

3.   **Create timeline.** Teachers establish a tentative time frame for implementing their action research plan. While trainers and coaches usually suggest some time for beginning practice, teachers are assured that they are not all expected to complete this Step 2 practice/coaching period at the same time or even at a set time. Learners know they will receive guidance from a more experienced leader throughout the process, regardless of the number of approximations they may need.

4.   **Collaborate.** Teachers work with peers who have experienced the same demonstrations, schedule peer observations to watch more experienced colleagues who have successfully implemented these demonstrations, and/or continue to work with their trainers or coaches to watch additional demonstrations and engage in individualized coaching based on personal needs.

When teachers begin to practice with children in real classroom situations, their skill, knowledge, judgment, and imagination are tested. Being absorbed in the messy business of untangling daily challenges for students is strenuous. It takes time to think, practice, and reflect on feedback and student work. As teachers are required to make decisions about their practice, they find themselves examining their existing beliefs, their commitments to change, and the probable consequences of their decisions for students. "Will my life really be improved if I do this?" becomes a daily refrain. The leader's decisive differentiation is instrumental to teachers' success during the "We Do" stage. Teachers often find themselves at lower developmental levels during the beginning stages of new learning. As the "We Do" phase progresses, they will be operating at a variety of levels on the learning continuum. Identifying and responding to those levels is the meat of the process for differentiation. Coaches must know when to give specific direction, when to set up collaborative pairs/teams, when to empathize and analyze, and when to remain silent.

A leader gains intimate knowledge of learners during Step 1, which translates into realistic expectations for Step 2. Think back to "Coach" Clark (chapter 4), who discovered in Step 1 that Barb was a bit of an outlaw who questioned the value of learning literacy strategies. Ms. Clark has set the expectation that all teachers will be adding some literacy to their content teaching. Now, in Step 2, she plans to work with Barb on the value-added aspect of weaving literacy tasks into her ELA curriculum work. Ms. Clark knows from the initial Step 1 conversations that not all the ELA teachers need this work but that in the case of this outlaw, it will help to move her into the settlement.

Revisiting some of Barb's colleagues on the middle school ELA team as they begin the move from the Step 1 demonstrations to the Step 2 practice and coaching, we see the kinds of decision making that go on at this stage. Teri, our veteran teacher, exclaims, "This is shaking up my beliefs! The dust is still settling around me. But I've decided to change the way I handle independent reading with my eighth-graders!"

Sam, the first-year teacher, comments on his struggles with organizing the content mandated by the state standards and the district curriculum. "I'm new to this grade level, and I'm still trying to figure out what to teach. I think I would benefit from some one-on-one time with 'Coach' before I'm able to move ahead."

Ms. Clark realizes that Sam is experiencing many of the common struggles of a first-year teacher. She decides that to help him focus more on the literacy aspects of his curriculum, they should spend some time together reviewing the action plan he has developed for his Step 2 practice. "Well, Sam, how are you feeling about the action plan you developed after our initial workshops last month?"

"To tell you the truth, I can't seem to get started with it. I'm too concerned with making sure that I'm teaching what's in the standards and curriculum. I'm really confused."

"The first year of teaching is loaded with change, obstacles, and confusion, so don't beat yourself up! Let's take another look at your action research plan, and I'm sure we can work out the bumps so that you can begin to try some of the literacy strategies you've identified."

"Okay, sounds good. Teri has been helping me a lot with getting to know the curriculum, and my mentor and I are focusing on that also."

"Great, because our work should be centered on the professional development goals the ELA team outlined. Remember that our goal was to implement a balanced approach to literacy in the middle school ELA curriculum. Our overall goal is to be giving the students literacy strategies, not simply teaching them books."

"Yeah, I remember the goals. I guess I'm still wondering how to get there. Maybe my action plan isn't very helpful."

After reflecting on the demonstrations in Step 1, Sam decides that as a first-year teacher he will need more time than some of the other team members for implementing literacy. He makes a few adjustments to his action research plan. First, he creates two questions for his students to focus on during the first semester: "What is the value of literacy?" and "What is reading?" He then sets up two times to observe Teri implement a reading strategy with her students. Sam also realizes his need for Coach Clark's help with grouping his students and gathering appropriate resources. With their continued conversations, Coach Clark helps Sam to believe not only in himself but also in his action research plan.

Val, the special educator who pushes into Teri's eighth-grade inclusion ELA class finds the team collaboration times to be very valuable. "Together, we have been able to plan for differentiation for my students who are not reading or writing on grade level. This kind of collaboration and leadership is changing our way of doing things—like using the whole-group format for teaching mini-lessons and then forming groups based on needs—and the students are getting better results from our practices."

Moving from demonstration to practice requires differing amounts of time, patience, and reflection for each adult learner. Perhaps the most vital part of "We Do" is the leader's compassion and humor in offering learners the freedom to approximate desired results. Learners need to have time to use new methods and to make decisions about what pieces of learning to implement and when and how they will do so. Reinforcing that "mistakes provide learning opportunities" and "there are no dumb questions" permits learners to live up to the professional development expectation that change will result from new learning.

Managing Discomfort

Attempting new strategies and practices inevitably brings discomfort. The early anticipation may wane quickly. Teacher leaders need to come to grips with the learners' discomfort as well as their own. The "We Do" sessions must reflect the needs and concerns of the implementers—the classroom teachers. In the following scenario, the members of a tenth-grade interdisciplinary team (ELA, science, social studies, math) had also expressed interest in a workshop to help them with their attempts to weave literacy into their content teaching. They had asked Marla, the high school literacy specialist, if she could present some strategies for them and then continue her support in their classrooms during her regularly scheduled push-in instruction. Marla agreed to present a daylong session for the team and then serve as the team members' coach throughout the semester as they implemented the strategies.

Now Marla has given the initial presentation (Step 1 demonstrations), and she and the teachers have gathered for a one-hour debriefing meeting. Let's listen in.

Carlos, a second-year ELA teacher, confesses that "it looked awesome, and you had such a convincing presentation, but right now I'm just trying to figure out how to get through one day at a time. I'll think about it a few more weeks before I try any of this stuff."

Mark, also an ELA teacher, laments to the group, "I can't imagine having time to 'do' literacy along with my content. Maybe I could do something on Fridays."

Eileen, a veteran math teacher, shares, "You all realize that I'm going to retire in two years. I'll help you in any way I can, but I am not going to spend my last days testing new ideas. My students do fine, and I'm not into changing now."

From their reflections, it seems that the demonstrations of beginning strategies have left some participants with little enthusiasm for doing the work. Their feedback leads our trainer/coach Marla to some significant decisions as she plans for Step 2 of the professional development. She knows that she will also need to schedule additional Step 1 demonstrations for some of these learners before they will be ready to begin to practice what they have seen. Marla thinks that perhaps Carlos and Mark will benefit from a few scheduled peer observations of colleagues from another team who are already implementing these strategies. As we will see in the following sections, coaching and differentiation will enable everyone to reap rewards from the initial anxiety.

Coaching: The Heart of "We Do"

Coaching is essential to adult learning. It provides the time and opportunity for learners to understand, interpret, and apply new strategies. It offers a means for transferring learning to classroom practice. The research is solid. The expectations are there. Learners are allowed to make as many approximations as needed. Coaches decide what is missing, what to target for continued modeling, when and if peer observations should begin, and what data to collect.

Coaching is the compassionate heart that ensures follow-up action in the classroom. While being coached, teachers agree on a focal point and on the desired effect for students. They explore their assumptions and the current reality of their classrooms. They generate alternative solutions to problems. They move at their own pace toward self-sufficiency with the new learning (McNeil & Klink, 2004). Every coaching meeting ends with "What's next?" Every new session begins with "Did we succeed with our next steps? Why? Why not?" Teacher and coach discuss what is working well and what needs to be revisited. We often remember, sometimes painfully, our errors for a long time. They impress us, and we feel beat up emotionally. The coach's job now is to offer encouragement and direction to turn disappointments into positive learning experiences.

Remember that in this differentiated framework of professional development, a district or school has many options for choosing leaders to coach. In many cases (as with the high school literacy specialist, Marla), the trainer from the original "I Do" demonstrations continues as the day-to-day coach during the "We Do" practice and coaching stage. This is possible because often these leaders already spend the majority of their day pushing in to support individual teachers as well as teams. At other times, a mentor who works primarily with teachers new to the profession is the person chosen to become the coach. For example, a school's speech teacher might be the perfect choice for presenting demonstrations of various strategies for teaching kindergarten students phonemic awareness. But the mentor might be the most logical person to step in at the "We Do" stage of practice and coaching to guide the new teachers who witnessed this presentation. Not every leader is capable of leadership at every stage of the differentiated framework. Districts and schools have to match the work to the worker and tap the leader most able to train, to facilitate, or to coach. (Chapter 3 will refresh your thinking about the roles of leaders within a school and district.)

The ultimate focus of coaching for teacher development is student learning. When the leaders are appropriately matched to the tasks and begin to coach, they become questioners, advisors, collaborators, learners, and observers. They engage in watching the action in classrooms. What is happening with the teacher learners when they return to the classrooms? Are they equipped to try new methods and prepared to gather student data to share at subsequent work sessions? Are they ready to engage in action research in their classrooms and to collaborate with others about what and how they are learning?

In *Powerful Designs for Professional Development*, Suzanne Bailey (2004, p. 252) states, "Relationships are the medium through which work happens." The coaching relationship is fragile and requires the coach to have not just a passion for the topic, but also a passion for the success of the person being coached. Great coaching is the result of the mutual commitment and action of teacher and learner as equal partners (McNeil & Klink, 2004). Jim Knight (2007, p. 33) has this to say about coaching:

- ✦ Coaching is about building relationships with teachers as much as it is about instruction. The heart of relationships is emotional connection.

- ✦ Instructional coaches adopt a partnership philosophy, which at its core means that they have an authentic respect for teachers' professionalism.

- ✦ The partnership philosophy is realized in collaborative work between the coach and the collaborating teacher.

- ✦ Instructional coaches model in the classroom so that teachers can see what correct implementation of an intervention looks like.

Differentiated Coaching

There are various approaches to coaching, and the type of coaching used depends on the learner's needs. Not every teacher will receive the same coaching arrangement, but all coaching will focus on the strategies that were demonstrated in the "I Do" stage workshop and that are reflected in the learner's action research plans.

Directive Coaching

Returning to the example of Carlos, the second-year teacher and member of the high school interdisciplinary team, let's envision that his mentor, Linda, had helped Marla with the initial literacy workshop training for his team. Since Linda is Carlos' mentor, it is decided that she will also serve as his coach in the "We Do" stage after the literacy workshop. Let's eavesdrop as we find coach and teacher huddled in the back of Carlos' classroom for their first post-workshop meeting.

"What is the most valuable thing you need me to do or say at this moment?" asks Linda.

"I need you to assure me that when I mess up if I attempt some of the literacy strategies Marla showed us, I'll still have my job. I need to see you do them with my classes. I need to see step by step over a few class periods how to do it."

Linda now assumes the role of a *directive* coach—not just a cheerleader, but the person who will help this teacher move from where he is to where he wants to be. Carlos has witnessed the demonstrations, been engaged in the learning process, and now has asked for specific guidelines on ways to proceed with his students. Directive coaching leads to success when a coach possesses the correct knowledge and skills and communicates in ways the new teacher can understand. The mentor/coach needs to be specific with language as he or she models. Direct questions will guide the coaching sessions to be sure that the new teacher's needs are being addressed. Linda begins by asking, "During the workshop, several strategies were demonstrated to help students use their literacy skills when reading. Which strategy would you like to try first? I know you can do this. Don't worry, together we'll find what works for you!"

"Well, I think my kids could really benefit from using 'fix-up' strategies while they are reading."

"Great!" says Linda, and together they co-plan a lesson that focuses on applying "fix-up" strategies when comprehension breaks down. Linda agrees to model what they have planned in Carlos' classroom the next day. She also creates a note-making guide for Carlos to use during the modeling lesson (see table 5.1, page 70). This guide includes:

+ A column for listing the important teaching behaviors the mentor engages in

+ A column to note what the students are doing during the teaching

+ A space for recording comments, questions, or insights gleaned while observing the model lesson

+ Spaces for both the mentor and the teacher to write reflections after the lesson is completed

Linda encourages Carlos to pay close attention during the lesson; to make notes about the specific language she uses to introduce and model the strategy; and to record some things he likes or doesn't like, some things he thinks work well, and anything he has trouble understanding. As Carlos observes the lesson, he should also try to notice whether his students are responding to the strategy.

Ideally, Linda and Carlos should collaborate to make the most efficient note-making guide for each model lesson. They will also work together to create a preliminary plan for Carlos to implement the strategy.

Finally, Linda and Carlos set a time to meet for a reflective talk after the lesson is modeled. Carlos will bring his notes and questions to this meeting, which will focus on his immediate needs and be customized to the daily challenge of helping his students use what they already know about literacy to tackle new content. Subsequent coaching sessions will include decisions about further modeling or co-teaching.

The next day, Linda models the lesson in Carlos' classroom. Then they meet at the appointed time to reflect on what took place. "Okay, Carlos, did we accomplish what we planned in our first meeting?"

Table 5.1: Note-Making Guide for Teachers

Teacher:	Date:
Coach:	Strategy/Issue:

Coach Behaviors	Student Behaviors

Teacher Observations/Questions	

Coach Reflections	Teacher Reflections

"I think so, because I just wanted to watch one 'fix-up' strategy, and the kids seemed to be getting the idea of using context to figure out unknown words pretty well. The pairs of students we put together were able to record correct definitions for the word list we provided. I have to admit that although the note-making guide we made was helpful, it was also a distraction. I couldn't keep up with what I was trying to record and listen to the kids talk at the same time. Could we work more on this before you model the next time?"

"It actually takes some time and practice to watch, listen, and record notes all at the same time. But we will pay attention to this when we work on our next guide and modeling session. What's next in terms of strategies for the kids? Do you remember any other 'fix-up' strategy you saw demonstrated that you think you are ready to try?"

Carlos is ready to review the list of strategies and have Linda help him decide what direction to take next. He is hoping to be able to teach a different strategy to each of his four groups of students, based on the groups' needs.

While this coaching relationship seems to be heading in the right direction, there is one more issue to be addressed. As a new member of a district that supports professional learning communities, Carlos is also struggling with his team role. Realizing how new roles and responsibilities can cause stress that slow the learning process, Linda contacts the team leader to share insights about Carlos' strengths and fears and arranges to accompany him to his next interdisciplinary team meeting.

Eileen, the veteran math teacher on this high school team, serves as the team leader and is conscious of the concerns newer teachers have when asked to share in team meetings. "Linda, I would welcome your coming to the meeting and supporting Carlos as he shares the literacy lesson with the team—and you may even be able to answer questions some of the rest of us have concerning literacy."

At the meeting, Linda observes and provides a supportive presence as Carlos shares his lesson with the team. The team members welcome him and give him validation, as well as some ideas for improving his next attempt. Eileen makes it clear that she has benefited from his presentation: "Thanks for the ideas of how to get the kids into the idea of fix-up strategies. I've been wondering how to explain that term 'fix-up,' and now I have some better ideas."

Mark shares his own experience with teaching the strategies: "I found that I needed to do a mini-lesson for the whole class and then provide time for pairs of students to practice some of the 'fix-up' strategies on short pieces of text."

This is an authentic, dynamic learning experience within a community of learners. Gradually, Carlos will grow professionally from the open communication and decreased isolation of the team time. He will benefit from having a safe haven for sharing points of view and challenging his own and others' thinking. He will be encouraged during problem-solving dialogue as the team grapples with questions.

Mentor teachers are in an excellent position to support new teachers in team meetings but should be careful not to put them in the position of seeming unprepared for the job. Mentors can maintain their support with a soft touch.

It takes considerable practice for new teachers to learn how to interact with veteran teachers. Eleanor Drago-Severson (2004, p. 21) points out that "adults with different ways of knowing experience the same events and situations in qualitatively different ways." Educators who are trainers and coaches "nee[d] to pay attention to the ways in which a learner is interpreting, or making meaning of, his or her experience, and then provide both supports and challenges that are developmentally appropriate to that way of making meaning" (p. 19). This quote reminds us of Ana and Scott, the two newly hired teachers from chapter 1 who attended the session on reading strategies and had two different reactions to the experience.

Directive coaching is designed to answer the immediate needs of the teachers who are being coached. Often the teachers identify their own needs, but sometimes they need the coaches' help to determine what to focus on. The coaches guide the teachers in acquiring skills that will enable them to solve problems and achieve goals on their own. Coaching will also help the teachers be prepared to engage in open-ended dialogue with their teams about alternative solutions to student problems.

Let's listen in on a directive coaching conversation between Carrie, a building coach, and Tyson, a physical education teacher, during a break in the teachers' lounge. They had both attended a professional development presentation by a numeracy leader from the high school staff. This was the first of several "I Do" demonstrations designed to acquaint the staff with formal and informal assessment tools that might be used for all high school disciplines.

Carrie initiates the conversation by asking Tyson, "What did you think about the speaker yesterday?"

Tyson admits, "I haven't figured out what he means. Am I supposed to start giving written quizzes or what?"

Carrie realizes that her friend is struggling with the idea of using a balance of formative and summative assessments to track student progress. She is careful not to tell her colleague what to do but rather engages him in a dialogue that provides an opportunity to continue asking questions. She begins by offering her definition of formative assessment: "I don't know about the quizzes, but I think the idea is to find ways to measure and track student progress during each lesson."

"You mean I have to evaluate each of the twenty-five to forty kids on the gym floor every day?"

"Well, let's look at what you are teaching right now. What unit are you doing with your tenth-graders this month?"

"Badminton. You know, how to serve and the basic rules. Then we learn about the smash and other shots."

"Okay, how do you know who is mastering all of this and who is not? What kind of assessment do you use now?"

"Well, day to day, I watch the kids. I move around to the groups as they practice and watch and tell them what they need to do differently."

"Great! That's a type of formative assessment. What else do you think you could do? Like the speaker said yesterday, 'Do you give your students a variety of ways to respond to their learning?' It sounds like performance is one of the ways you can assess. What else is there?"

"I honestly don't know. That's a lot of kids on the gym floor. They have a lot more physical freedom in the gym than they do in a classroom. The noise level is always an obstacle, and I've got kids who don't even want to be there. I'm not sure what to do other than show them how to do something and then have them try it. Then I try to help those who aren't very successful. Model, observe, and give feedback. That's what I do."

"Okay. I think you should keep doing all that, and I see your point about the number of kids and the noise. The day-to-day or even moment-by-moment assessment might be a bit easier in the classroom than in the gym. Have you ever thought about using the pair-share strategy that we used in the faculty meeting last month?"

"You mean when we talked to the person sitting next to us before we shared out ideas with the whole group?"

"Yes, that's the one. I was thinking that if you already have the kids in teams or practice groups, you could give them a few specific ideas or questions to discuss with another person in their group, and then each group could throw out an idea for everyone to hear."

"I never thought of that working with a large bunch of kids. But, you know, it might work. That way, I could sort of force the kids who don't pay attention or just fool around to focus, and their partner might get them involved. With some practice, the kids might like the change of pace it would provide. Would you be able to help me write up a lesson with the pair-share included and then come to one of my classes next week and help me give it a try?"

"Sure, let's set some times. I'm thinking that you might just use the pair-share with some of the groups as you are traveling around observing. You might not even use it with everyone. Let's plan it a few different ways and see what works with the kids."

"I'll give it a shot! I'll also have to come up with a way to keep track of how and if this makes any difference in my knowing who knows what."

This coach identified her colleague's immediate need to begin to implement more formative assessments. Their conversation exhibited each person's respect for the other's professionalism. Carrie communicated in a way that established an emotional connection, which allowed each person to listen to the other. In directive coaching, it is the job of the coach to offer choice, support, and enough information that the person being coached is able to make a decision. Carrie was willing to give time and patience to make it as easy as possible for her colleague to attempt a new strategy.

Collaborative Coaching

As teachers, teacher leaders, and professional developers cement their relationships, they are ready to engage in *collaborative* coaching. Collaborative coaching provides opportunities for joint problem-solving and is usually quite effective when coaches are working with more veteran teachers who may not always be open to change. Let's return to our interdisciplinary team of high school teachers who were exploring strategies for reading in the content area with their coach, Marla. We recall that Mark was not convinced that anyone could "do" literacy without sacrificing content. Let's assume that Mark and Marla have been colleagues for several years and have developed a level of trust in each other that lends itself to a collaborative approach. While Mark does not need directive coaching, he is very open to solving problems jointly.

Marla asks Mark for a time to chat. When they meet, the coaching begins with Marla suggesting that they create a list of the pros and cons of focusing on literacy strategies in an English language arts classroom. Through this collaboration, Marla and Mark come to agree that literacy is a tool that all learners need but do not always have. During their conversation, Mark reveals that while he understands and agrees that students need more literacy instruction, his problem is time. He needs to teach his content. How will he find the time to "do literacy"?

Collaborative coaching helps these colleagues jointly explore possible solutions to the time-versus-content issue. They decide to co-plan and co-teach a lesson that employs an anticipation guide related to the novel that Mark's students are currently studying. The anticipation guide is designed to focus students on literacy skills and, at the same time, prepare them for the character changes that will occur within the next chapter. As part of their "We Do" collaborating, Mark and Marla agree to journal about their co-teaching experience and to reflect the following week, concentrating on the literacy aspect of their lesson. Marla suggests that their reflections focus on two main questions: Did their plan for weaving literacy into content promote student skills in both content and literacy? Did the literacy work mean sacrificing time for content discussion? The answers to these questions will determine the course of their future teamwork. These colleagues are now set on a coaching path that will build capacity for implementing other strategies demonstrated during the initial "I Do" literacy workshop.

Sharing the Learning With the Team

Now let's follow Mark as he attends a weekly team meeting after his work with Marla. All of the team members are engaged in the "We Do" stage, having enjoyed some type of coaching. The agenda for this meeting has teachers sharing a successful lesson and bringing student work samples that provide evidence of learning. Mark begins by sharing the anticipation guides that three of his students completed. "I want my students to appreciate how authors incorporate character changes in order to add interest and complexity to literature. With Marla's help, I introduced my students to anticipation guides. I liked the idea of presenting them with a *before*-reading strategy. In these anticipation guides, I asked them to read a series of statements about the novel's characters and agree or disagree with each statement before reading the assigned pages."

Carlos asks, "I'm wondering how your struggling readers made out with this. Did you find that they could better understand what they were reading after filling out the guide?"

Mark replies, "Well, I think so, but I'd like you guys to look at my samples and see if you agree that this has been successful." He then passes out three samples of a follow-up assignment in which students were asked to respond to a journal prompt about the reading they had done after completing the anticipation guides. The team members look at the samples and find that all three students have used information gleaned from the text to support their responses, either adequately or with considerable detail.

Carlos is impressed. "I'm having trouble choosing which of these samples is from a struggling reader. All these papers look really good. Can you give me some ideas on creating anticipation guides for my students?"

Mark agrees to work with Carlos and a few other interested members of the team to construct guides for their students, and the team agrees to look at these team members' student work samples at the next meeting. Mark also states that he is going to continue developing literacy strategies for his students with Marla. The team expresses curiosity in hearing about that work in future team meetings. Mark's reciprocal coaching time has put him in a good position to be a successful collaborator with others. He is actively engaged in the "We Do" of professional development by taking on more responsibility for his own learning and sharing it with others for the benefit of students.

Collaborative coaching leads to more co-teaching and eventual peer observations among the team members. Collaborative coaching may be practiced from time to time or over a span of years, depending on district initiatives and individual needs.

Nondirective Coaching

Perhaps Eileen, our veteran high school math teacher who is close to retirement, will benefit from *nondirective* coaching. Nondirective coaching is learner directed and of great value to teachers who have spent several years teaching and are engaged in job-embedded professional development. If a teacher wishes to be an active and equal partner with a coach, then nondirective coaching usually works very well. With this type of coaching, the coach and the teacher must agree on the desired outcome of the coaching. Then the coach helps the teacher to understand the thinking processes that can lead to that outcome (McNeil & Klink, 2004).

As a career comes to a close, a teacher needs validation of past efforts but is also expected to continue to participate in the new learning initiatives of the district. In nondirective coaching, it is important to identify any assumptions that might be hindering a teacher from implementing strategies. Eileen is cooperative and willing to collaborate but hesitant to spend time on new techniques. Marla, Eileen's coach, learns more about Eileen's apprehensions in their first meeting. Since the majority of Eileen's students have always passed her course, and since she accepts that there will always be failures in a class, she feels there is no need to make any adjustments: "If it works, why fix it?"

Of course, no one can be forced into a coaching situation, but Eileen has already agreed to work with her team colleagues on a group action research plan of adding more literacy to their content teaching, so the idea of a coaching relationship with Marla is acceptable to her. The key to nondirective coaching is to establish purpose. Marla and Eileen agree to explore the idea of assumptions and the role they play in teaching.

Guided by Marla, Eileen develops a list of her current beliefs about students' use of literacy as a tool for learning. Next, she generates a list of the literacy strategies she is currently teaching, such as figuring out unknown words through the understanding of prefixes. She also produces a list of literacy skills that students *should* master, such as being able to set a purpose for their reading. Several meetings later, after she has been given adequate time and space for thinking, Eileen writes a "big" question on a chart: "Am I doing everything I can to help all my students master the skills of literacy?"

Looking at her coach, Eileen quietly acknowledges that by assuming that there would be failures, she has been allowing failure in her classroom. She slowly recognizes her current reality by exploring her assumptions about student learning. As a result, the purposes of the initial demonstrations in the "I Do" stage become clear. Eileen wants and will expect better results from her students as she practices new strategies with the help of Marla's coaching. A new list is born: a list of strategies to enable Eileen to weave literacy teaching into her current content teaching. Continued meetings, co-planning, modeling, and persistent reflection will lead to renewed action in her classroom.

As did Carlos and Mark, Eileen takes her new ideas and practices to her team meetings. She has many opportunities to share her lists and her thinking about which literacy strategies students should be learning. She and Mark spend time planning a few mini-lessons to try in their math and ELA classes. After having used the mini-lessons, they bring student work samples such as journal responses, exit tasks, and quizzes to the team meetings. The resultant sharing and decision making have a transformational impact not just on Eileen's teaching but on that of her entire team.

The nondirective coaching style has taught Eileen that sometimes assumptions can hinder progress, even if the end results were previously considered acceptable. Without this experience, Eileen might have ended her career without ever having understood the value of examining assumptions and then acting on what she learned.

Watching the Action

Without coaching support during the "We Do" stage, none of the teachers in these scenarios would have successfully implemented what they saw demonstrated in the "I Do" stage. Teacher learning reaches its potential when teachers observe and work together. Peer observations illuminate aspects of performance never noticed during most administrator observations. They establish the basis for improvements in teacher practice. During "We Do," coaches watch teachers, teachers watch other teachers, disciplines watch other disciplines, grades levels watch other grade levels, and administrators watch as the power of differentiation permeates their culture.

CHAPTER 6

Responsibility and Use: "You Do"

As we move into Step 3: "You Do," it is a good time to remember that the three-step model of differentiated job-embedded professional development is not intended as a formula for anyone to replicate exactly or specifically. The model does contain certain components within each of the three steps, but it is the people—the leaders and the learners—who make the decisions as to what will be attended to and finally internalized, and how and when the learning will be accomplished.

When thinking about "You Do," one should focus on the notion of responsibility. The teacher leaders have the responsibility for providing significant demonstrations within a risk-free environment of expectations for the learners. They don't dictate the path of learning but rather, beginning with the "I Do" stage, clearly signal the expectation that the learning will ultimately be accomplished. According to Brian Cambourne (1988, p. 37), the learners have two responsibilities: "Firstly, [the learner] is expected to become proficient in the total act; this is not negotiable—he *must* eventually learn. Secondly, he is expected to make decisions about the most useful aspect with which to engage from the demonstration which he is currently experiencing." In other words, teacher learners can decide, and take the responsibility for, which of the demonstrated strategies they will attempt to add to their teaching repertoires and when they will do so. The learner chooses how to attempt the eventual learning and is allowed as many approximations as needed during the "We Do" stage.

We empower teacher learners when we offer this combination of choice and expectation. The majority of adult learners flourish under these conditions and strive to meet and even go beyond the expectations of others. By the time they enter this stage of their learning, the teachers who have gradually taken on responsibility have become empowered by:

+ Thriving on their ability to use demonstrations and peer collaboration to assist learning

+ Making valuable decisions as to what parts of the learning to attempt first and how to start this learning

+ Making first attempts and then seeking help

+ Allowing themselves to be coached by more knowledgeable colleagues

The responsibility of "You Do" brings to mind the words from Shel Silverstein's poem "This Bridge": "This bridge will only take you halfway there—the last few steps you'll have to take alone" (1981, p. 169). Learners now stand at the brink, feeling self-reliant and ready to walk alone. They have been cheered, supported, and guided by those who have gone before them. Leaders stand near the end of the bridge and watch as the learners take those last steps, relying on their own passion and skill.

An Evolutionary Process

Leaders and coaches do not pronounce learners "ready" for Step 3. Instead, "You Do" is an evolutionary process. All the teachers who have been introduced in the preceding chapters are evolving into this "You Do" stage of learning. They are not in the same place, do not have the same results from students, and are not necessarily teaching the same strategies in classrooms on the same days. Although groups of them began the "I Do" step together, in most cases they are no longer together for the "You Do" stage. Their diversity has necessitated different paths along the way to learning. They have each been progressing at their own pace along the continuum of the original expectations set during Step 1. They will all, as Cambourne says, "become proficient in the total act" with guidance and continued use of the demonstrations they have been provided.

The "You Do" step is the transition from *not knowing* to *knowing*. While "We Do" is like walking through the center of chaos, "You Do" provides a feeling of calm. Coaches have gradually released responsibility for learning, enabling teachers to systematically own new strategies. Teachers have faced many apprehensions and worked through obstacles to take on full responsibility for their learning. Action research within teams has answered questions relevant to the teachers' daily work. The role of the coach now becomes one of celebration with the learners. Goals have been met. Teams have transformed. Most importantly, students have gained more expertise. Teacher leaders and coaches can now begin the journey through the differentiated "I Do, We Do, You Do" framework once again, introducing new demonstrations, setting new expectations, and reinforcing or restructuring coaching relationships based on learner needs.

Listening in on Teacher Reflection

Let's revisit our sample teachers from previous chapters and reflect with them on their differentiated journeys. Once again we find Carlos, the second-year teacher, huddled with Linda, his mentor, and engaged in animated dialogue. The young teacher is confident and proud of the work his students are doing. "You said we would find the way together, and that was the key for me. I knew that I was expected to accomplish new methods, but I was so overwhelmed. You really helped me with your modeling. Knowing that I could rely on having as much time as I needed to practice with your feedback made a world of difference. It's only been a few months, but I'm actually feeling more like a 'real' teacher. I'm proud of my abilities and the success of my students. I even think I know what you can help me with next!"

As Carlos generates this important information, he puts his focus on the process as well as the product. Independent learners become skillful at self-evaluation. They know how they learn and can initiate the next steps for personal growth. It is these statements that exhibit success and give a mentor/coach validation of learner growth. Linda is assured that Carlos is evolving into the Step 3 of independent "You

Do" teaching. She leaves Carlos with a hug and a very important statement: "I'm proud of you! I'll see you next Tuesday to begin our next challenge."

A conversation between Marla, the coach, and Mark, her colleague who struggled to add new methods to his content-pressured day, also sounds promising. "I never really believed that we would have been able to work on this for so long. Most of my previous experience with professional development never included time to try strategies coupled with comfortable feedback. I think you really wanted me to succeed, and you were not going to give up on me. Reflecting in our journals gave us the thinking necessary for every new conversation. This was absolutely invaluable to me. I hope you are ready for more of this!"

"Absolutely! As your partner looking for answers, I also found the journaling to be very valuable. Thank you for believing in this coaching concept and giving it your all." Once again, this conversation signals to the coach that a teacher is moving into the "You Do" stage of learning.

Visiting the soon-to-retire teacher, Eileen, we find her engaging in a similar conversation with Marla. "I know that you thought about me not as an individual who needed to be fixed but as one who needed to be coached in a new direction. I appreciated and took comfort in the knowledge that I could move at my own speed and make decisions based on my students' needs and accomplishments. You spent time, you showed patience, you endured my frustrations, and you smiled and talked to me. We watched my kids and we tossed around choices and methods that might make a difference in their quality of work. Rather than asking the questions, you encouraged me to ask the questions that I really needed to ask in order to deepen my thinking. This journey was about us moving me to a better place in my teaching, even though I was at the end of my career." We see another teacher showing grateful enthusiasm for her differentiated journey and her ability to step into the "You Do" stage of learning.

Remember our middle school ELA team? Coach Clark differentiated with great care to bring Barb the outlaw into the settlement with Teri, Val, Carole, and Sam. Even as Sam spends more time in the "We Do" of approximation, the others are crossing over the bridge to independent use of at least some of the new learning. Their opportunities to come together before teaching to plan lessons and then to regroup after teaching have enabled and encouraged them to examine their beliefs, methods, interventions, and assessments. Change is difficult, and change is slow. Reaching independent success in the midst of change depends on teamwork, coaching, and collaborative problem-solving. "We are becoming a team of individuals capable of learning and growing together as we focus on improving our skills and building routines that strengthen student skills," Barb reports proudly. "And we had many opportunities during this semester to co-plan and co-teach with Coach Clark after our initial workshop demonstrations."

Teri agrees and adds, "I think we all benefited from the debriefing sessions we had as a team after we did the teaching together."

"I certainly have a lot more to learn, but at least now I understand what our principal means when he says we need a 'balanced literacy' approach," shares Sam. "Every time I came to your room, Teri, I left a new man! Watching you in action brought meaning to the terms *read-aloud* and *shared reading*. Thanks!"

Carole, as the new member of the team, expresses her gratitude for everyone's support and validation of her existing knowledge of balanced literacy. "I felt like I was teaching you and learning from you at the same time. Things are different at the middle school level, but having this time together and teaming to solve problems was wonderful."

Leaders' Follow-Up

Those who have led others to the final step of independence will now continue to check in with their colleagues to monitor their learning and make adjustments when needed. With the differentiated framework firmly in place, new initiatives will be identified and planned. When a coach walks alongside a colleague in Step 3, he or she should always remember to:

+ Celebrate every success, no matter how small

+ Respond as a co-learner

+ Assist without making suggestions

+ Act as a resource

+ Remain nonjudgmental and confidential

Results of the Differentiated Framework

The National Staff Development Council (2009b, homepage) asks all districts to be certain that "every educator engages in effective professional learning every day so every student achieves." While this practice seems to be common sense, there is much work to be done. School districts must do more than mandate professional development in an effort to raise student test scores. They must construct a strong framework around differentiation. When learner motivation, interest, readiness, and background experiences are ignored, the learners themselves are ignored. Learning is not about performing a specific task in a specific amount of time under a specific set of circumstances. Learning is about growth, change, and the relationship between one person and another. When a learner realizes how to ask for feedback, the responsibility for the learning is acknowledged. The more responsibility learners take on, the more they seek the conversations they need, not what others think they need. The prolonged interaction of coaches and learners has a positive effect not just on the staff of a district, but ultimately on the quality of student work.

The teachers from our earlier scenarios have begun taking the last few magical steps. Their chances for independence have been enhanced by professional development options designed to be specific to individual needs while still moving groups of teachers forward with district initiatives. These teachers have enjoyed respectful and nurturing relationships with coaches. They have received ample demonstrations and have been strongly connected to the expected learning through engagement. They have been motivated and inspired by the work of others. Differentiated professional development for these learners has turned theory into classroom practice that actually works. The teachers not only understand the term *differentiation* but also have experienced the *feel* of differentiation.

Drawing an analogy between differentiated professional development and gardening might further our understanding of how this process works. The seeds of differentiation are scattered during the demonstrations of "I Do." It is not a given that anything will sprout and flourish, but the teacher leader, like the gardener, observes intently in order to know what is needed to guide each seed to life.

"We Do" is a time of patient nurturing, coaxing, and waiting. The learning is shaped to the specific needs of the learner, just as a seedling is exposed to exactly the right amount of sun and water over time. This is a phase of tentative beginnings and many false starts. The teacher leader often has to give more demonstrations, just as the gardener may have to plant new seeds and use different combinations of water and other nutrients. Teacher leader and gardener both must be fully engaged in the process to ensure their charges' will to thrive. Some learners grow steadily, as do certain plants. Others must be given specialized support, creative management with persistent attention, to find the exact route to flourish on their own.

Ultimately, the teacher leader and gardener reap the rewards of patience and time: the teachers transfer their new learning to their classrooms; the beauty and fragrance of flowers in full bloom fill the garden. "You Do" is a time of joyful celebration, a time to savor success and share proven techniques with others.

The ability to self-reflect and initiate one's own future learning is the product of the "You Do" stage. The release of responsibility for learning has made the final shift. Although not all learners take the last few steps together or at the same time, differentiation is what makes independence a reality. Districts that offer an "I Do, We Do, You Do" framework within a professional learning community can produce genuine learning for both adults and students. When a differentiated structure becomes part of a culture, professional development brings the promise of significant, lasting changes in adult habits in the classroom. Teacher learning that increases achievement for all students is sustainable through differentiation. This is one way that districts widen their leadership capacity to ensure continuous learning for teachers, administrators, and students. Differentiated professional development offers learners a series of opportunities that create a cycle of steady growth, making success possible for all teachers, regardless of their beginning knowledge.

CHAPTER 7

Teacher Leaders as Mentors and Team Facilitators

In the preceding chapters, we discussed the power of using in-house experts to deliver professional development in a differentiated manner through the "I Do, We Do, You Do" model. The peer coaching and daily availability of expertise that result in the embedding of best-practice strategies in each teacher's classroom are the epitome of colleague-to-colleague support. In our descriptions of the coaching process, we touched on two other professional development vehicles that are driven by peer support: mentoring for new teachers and collaborative team meetings. In this chapter, we will deepen our discussion of the role of teacher leaders in providing these opportunities for differentiated job-embedded professional growth.

Teacher Leaders as Mentors

The guidance and support of colleagues is crucial as new teachers enter the teaching profession and adapt to the culture of each individual school. Culture and expectations go beyond the statements in teacher handbooks. Colleague-to-colleague support has always been and will remain an important guide through the maze of that challenging first year. When colleagues pitch in to support their new team member as they move together through the challenges and protocols of each school day, they provide an informal type of mentoring.

All of us can recall those special colleagues who supported us during our careers, especially at the outset. They were teachers who, even before the advent of PLCs, shared their support freely and were our mentors before mentoring became a recognized position. This "on the job training" was powerful. When we needed support, we knew where to turn. We listened to the master teachers' stories and revered those stories as the way that teaching should be.

In no way do we want to minimize the power and value of these fond memories. However, the danger of the unofficial mentorship model was that districts had little systemic influence on the stories being shared. There was no consistency of message, no shared vision and direction. Master teachers' stories were based on their personal beliefs, values, and experiences.

Today, many school districts have adopted a formal mentoring program that consists of matching new teachers with a veteran mentor. Sometimes referred to as a buddy system, this model of mentoring reminds one of the big brother/big sister relationship from freshman year in college. Sometimes the pairings work; other times they falter. In *New Teacher Induction: How to Train, Support, and Retain New Teachers* (2003), Annette Breaux and Harry Wong compare this approach to a blind date. It is a question of relationship building, and the rapport between the mentor and mentee is crucial.

The buddy model is fraught with challenges, one of which can be the diverse personalities and philosophies within the cadre of mentors. In *Coaching and Mentoring First-Year and Student Teachers*, India Podsen and Vicki Denmark acknowledge this challenge: "Now, here is the dilemma: Enthusiasm for mentoring has not been supported by a clearly defined purpose for mentoring and the training needed to support mentors" (2000, p. 4). Mentors may be excited to embrace the role of mentor for their new colleagues, but without extensive professional development that deals with adult learning theory, peer coaching, and the key tenets of the mentoring role, the best-intentioned mentoring team may inadvertently transmit an array of mixed messages. This can be very confusing to new teachers, and the confusion will weaken the impact of the mentoring program. Worse yet, mixed messages may lead to misinterpretations of the goals and philosophy of the district, thus weakening the PLC instead of strengthening it.

Full-Time Mentors

We suggest that this fragmentation of message and delivery can be avoided by establishing an *induction program that is facilitated by a mentor* (or team of mentors for larger districts). In such programs, the mentors are teacher leaders who are released from their teaching duties to assume the role of mentor. Mentoring is their sole responsibility. In smaller districts, one districtwide mentor is able to support teachers throughout the district. In larger districts, there is a choice of having a cadre of districtwide mentors or of placing a mentor in each school. This is partly a financial decision, dependent on how many mentors the budget can support. (Title IIA is a possible funding source.) The key is not the quantity of mentors but rather the consistency of message that the mentors deliver. In the case of school-based mentors, it is crucial that the district's team of mentors be trained together and meet frequently both for collaborative problem solving and to ensure that they are in sync with supporting the mission, vision, goals, and values of the district.

Full-time mentors are in an ideal position to provide differentiated job-embedded professional development. Based on classroom visits with each new teacher, they can identify individual needs and offer cycles of "I Do, We Do, You Do" learning in a nonevaluative, risk-free setting. They are available to model and co-teach as necessary.

Mentoring is a daunting task, yet one that can reap powerful benefits for a professional learning community. Mentors must be selected with great care. They must be veteran teachers who walk the talk of the PLC. They must have a record of embedding the best practices from the district's professional development initiatives in their daily practice as classroom teachers and be regarded by their colleagues as master teachers. Actions always speak louder than words. Mentors must be recognized as avid supporters of the professional learning community's mission, vision, values, and goals. Thus, administrators and/or the interview team must look to established teacher leaders when selecting mentors. They are the keepers of a professional learning community's stories; they have helped to build the culture. They, in turn, are best suited to share those stories with the PLC's newest members.

The importance of prior knowledge has been established as key in all learning experiences. Each mentee will face challenges on the journey through the first years of teaching. When mentors bring an array of professional and life experiences to the role, the authenticity of their guidance and support is enhanced. Podsen and Denmark (2000, p. 4) emphasize that mentoring is

> a sustained relationship between a novice and an expert. In a clearly defined teacher-mentoring relationship, the expert provides help, support, and guidance that helps the novice develop the necessary skills to enter or continue on his career path. As a mentor, you have two main roles, as an expert and as a role model, in your teaching field.

Mentors' ability to differentiate their support for each mentee is contingent on the diverse strategies in their pedagogical toolboxes.

No one path leads an educator to the role of teacher mentor, but prior experience as a teacher leader contributes to any mentor's effectiveness. Having previously earned the respect of colleagues paves the way for a relationship based on trust in the mentor's efficacy. One example is Monique, a literacy specialist who decided to change positions and become a teacher mentor as a final step in her career. Since colleagues already recognized her as an expert in literacy instruction, her coaching was accepted with enthusiasm. Veteran teachers knew that she had achieved great success in her role as a literacy coach, and they shared those stories with their new teammates. As a literacy specialist and teacher leader, she had already facilitated professional development. In short, her reputation opened doors of trust that a less-experienced colleague could not open as easily.

Next, consider Xavier, a teacher in his late forties who transitioned to a mentor position after many years as a classroom teacher. His rapport with colleagues and students was well established. The segue from a respected role as a collaborative team leader to that of teacher mentor was seamless. He transferred the skills that he had applied over the years helping new teachers as a team leader to his expanded role as a full-time mentor.

In both of these cases, the mentors were able to build on their established reputations as master teachers and their roles as leaders in their professional learning communities. They carried their enthusiasm for their PLCs into the mentoring role and served as active models of their districts' mission, vision, values, and goals.

But is it feasible for one mentor to meet the needs of an entire school or district? One might ask if it is possible for a districtwide mentor to possess the subject-matter skills necessary to support K–12 teachers from all departments and grade levels. We would argue, based on our research and experience, that the challenges for new teachers are not subject-matter oriented. In the few cases where subject-matter deficiencies exist, other teacher leaders may provide support. Typically, new teachers need support and mentoring in classroom management, lesson planning, the essentials of good teaching, and life skills for interacting in a collaborative culture. Mentors who have been recognized as experts in best practices in classroom instruction are able to provide the needed support for any grade level or discipline.

It is imperative that mentees view their mentor as a master of pedagogy and a true believer in ongoing learning. If the mentor does not walk the talk of the professional learning community and model best-practice instruction as part of the process, then the mentees will lose faith in the process, as well as in the person. Mentoring is perhaps the single most important example of the impact of teacher leaders on a PLC. Just as kindergarten is the foundation of a child's view of school, the first year of teaching is the launchpad for the professional journey of each teacher. Mentors are the first and best chance of ensuring a successful launch that will set teachers on a positive trajectory.

In earlier chapters, we saw how teacher leaders acculturate new teachers to a PLC through coaching and differentiated professional development. The role of mentor is a logical fit with that of professional developer. Sharon Feiman-Nemser, Cynthia Carver, Sharon Schwille, and Brian Yusko (1999, p. 10) point out that "support without development leaves teacher learning to chance." Breaux and Wong (2003, p. 63) state that "what a new teacher needs is a teacher or a tutor." When the "I Do" and "We Do" stages of professional development are presented by the mentor, the trust from the established rapport between mentor and mentees strengthens the impact of the learning. The richness of the experience is enhanced with the mentor in the teaching role, modeling and working alongside colleagues to help them grow professionally. It is this expansion from the traditional supportive "buddy" model of mentoring to the mentor as a coach that places induction at the heart of a PLC's culture of job-embedded learning. Whether in established workshops or in the on-the-spot sharing that is differentiated to meet each new teacher's needs on a day-to-day basis, the mentor's modeling and support provide a resource that is unrivaled.

Teacher Leaders as Team Facilitators

In *Teacher Leadership That Strengthens Professional Practice*, Charlotte Danielson states that, "arguably, the most critical skill for a teacher leader is the ability to facilitate dialogue among teachers" (2006, p. 134). In a PLC, collaborative teams are an important venue for such dialogue and for colleague-to-colleague support. Much has been written about the value of collaborative teams that meet regularly to align curriculum, analyze student work, and make data-driven decisions about next steps. As Richard DuFour and Robert Eaker state in *Professional Learning Communities at Work*, "Building a school's capacity to learn is a collaborative rather than an individual task. People who engage in collaborative team learning are able to learn from one another, thus creating momentum to fuel continued improvement" (1998, p. 27). In *Revisiting Professional Learning Communities at Work*, collaboration is defined as "a *systematic* process in which people work together, *interdependently*, to analyze and *impact* professional practice in order to improve individual and collective results" (DuFour et al., 2008, p. 464).

Michael Fullan (1997, p. 41) has emphasized the importance of expanding the role of teacher leaders to aid collaboration: "The key issues as I see them are twofold: to broaden the leadership roles of more and more teachers while reshaping the culture of the school [to produce] built-in collaboration involving all (or the majority of) teachers." Teacher leadership of grade-level or departmental teams makes it easier to establish norms and provides on-the-spot facilitation of differentiated collaboration. While administrators oversee the "big picture," teacher leaders guide their colleagues to the defined goals for their specific team.

Let's see how this works by envisioning a middle school social studies team that is reviewing data from a recent common assessment. All seventh-grade students have written a document-based essay. Social studies teachers from all seventh-grade teams have scored the essays using a common rubric. For their collaboration time, the team members have come prepared to share their data and to look at examples of student work. Interesting discussions develop as teachers reflect on the achievement of their students vis-à-vis the grade-level data.

The team leader, Ms. Gaynor, challenges her team to examine the students' work to identify strengths and gaps in performance. She asks clarifying questions to keep the discussion focused. "Our data report shows that many of our students scored well, while others wrote weaker essays. Our task today is to examine student work. Are there any strategies that are prevalent in the higher-scoring essays? Or do you note any strategies that are lacking in many of the weaker essays?"

Kathleen observes that her students bring strong background knowledge to their essays but lack organizational skills. Stan reflects that students in his class all use a common graphic organizer to gather information from the documents, but their essays show little knowledge beyond what is contained in the documents themselves. Being accustomed to working in a culture of collaboration, Kathleen "borrows" the graphic organizer from Stan, while he explores strategies for connecting students' prior knowledge to the task at hand.

Team leader Gaynor then challenges the team members from grades 6 and 8 to find connections that they can use either to prepare students (grade 6) or to provide follow-up support (grade 8). The sixth-grade social studies teachers conclude that they could begin using some common organizational tools so that all students would enter grade 7 with the same strategies in their toolboxes, allowing the seventh-grade teachers to tap this prior knowledge and build forward. Grade 8 teachers decide to share several anonymous examples of the seventh-grade essays with their students, asking them to identify strengths and gaps using a process similar to the one the team just employed. Through active engagement, students would transfer strategies to their own practice, thus addressing any instructional gaps from the prior year's curriculum.

Through purposeful discussion and targeted facilitation, this middle school team has identified strengths and gaps using the data from the seventh-grade common assessment. Although the data are more "personal" for the seventh-grade teachers, Ms. Gaynor's facilitation of the discussion has resulted in action plans for the teachers at all three grade levels, which can be further addressed at the team's future curriculum update meetings.

When teachers collaborate to pool their skills and knowledge around the same goal, everyone benefits. As Stephanie Hirsh and Joellen Killion put it, "When teachers work collaboratively, build on one another's experiences, and use those experiences as a source of learning, they have the potential to meet nearly every challenge they face related to teaching and learning" (2007, p. 87). The teachers in this middle school story have had an opportunity to both share expertise and learn from colleagues. As a result of their collaboration, they will return to their classrooms prepared to better support their students' learning.

Teamwork may not always be accomplished so smoothly. Personal dynamics may come into play, making collaboration a challenge. For instance, the makeup of a team may include teachers who do not value collaboration and feel forced to participate. A new teacher may feel threatened by veterans who are set in their ways and be reluctant to ask questions or share opinions. However, when team leaders clearly establish purpose and keep the emphasis on positively impacting student learning, teams are able to work their way through the growing pains of team building.

Using teacher leaders to facilitate team discussions focused on improving student achievement allows professional development to be differentiated to meet the needs of each team. In *Results Now*, Mike Schmoker asserts that "if there is anything that the research community agrees on, it is this: The right kind of continuous, structured teacher collaboration improves the quality of teaching and pays big, often immediate, dividends in student learning and professional morale in virtually any setting" (2006, p. 177). When teachers are able to voice their individual needs within a risk-free learning community, they appreciate the value of differentiation.

Let's listen in as Ms. Shaw, a teacher leader, facilitates a grade-5 collaborative team meeting. She opens on a positive note: "Our agenda item for today is to review the data from the social studies assessment that we scored together last week. First of all—let's have a group high-five for exceeding our SMART [strategic and specific, measurable, attainable, results-oriented, timebound] goal! We were shooting for 80 percent at mastery and we hit 85 percent! Go team!

"Today our task is to look at the item analysis for the multiple-choice section. We agreed to look at all items where 90 percent or more of our students responded correctly and all items where less than 75 percent of our students had the correct answer. Our goals are (1) to celebrate our successes so that we can continue to embed successful strategies and (2) to identify our areas of need so that we can either revisit our curriculum map or access any professional development that would help to support our program. We have the printout from our instructional technology department, so let's go down the list and pick out the first item with over 90 percent success."

Levar quickly responds, "Look at item number 11! Ninety-nine percent of our students had that right. Let's look at the question. Oh—it was about the Erie Canal, and our fourth-grade curriculum nails that topic! We need to share that celebration at next week's vertical team meeting."

This dialogue continues until the teachers have identified all of the strengths and logged them so that they can be shared with colleagues from all grade levels. Then the process moves on to the identification of the areas of need.

Pat sees a red flag. "Yikes! Look at item 14! Only 45 percent of our students got that one right. That was the question on *urban* and *rural*. I was worried about that one—I don't think I used those terms at all in with my class."

Chris notices something interesting. "But look! All of the students in Vicki's class got that one right. Vicki! What's up?"

"Guess it was my lucky day! The week before, I was reading a story during read-aloud time that used those exact terms. We stopped and talked about them and brainstormed places that we know that are urban and others that are rural."

Ms. Shaw offers her analysis. "So, it looks like a vocabulary issue. Those words are on the state's key vocabulary list, so we will need to revisit our curriculum map. It appears that we have a gap in the alignment of our program with the state's core curriculum. I'll put that on the agenda for our next release day, and we may identify other agenda items as we continue today's discussion."

Chris laments, "I know that I slipped up on actively using all of the vocabulary from the state's list in my teaching. I could have used *urban* and *rural* just as easily as *city* and *country*."

Vicki suggests, "We could all use the read-aloud book. It's a great story, and I also have an extension writing task that I'd be happy to share on release day."

Ms. Shaw speaks again. "So here is an 'aha' for us. Pat, since you will be attending the building-wide social studies vertical team meeting on Friday, would you please share that we all need to revisit the state's established vocabulary list so that the key terms for each grade level are used in all classrooms? I remember that when we were looking at the last common assessment for math, we discovered a similar vocabulary issue. Perhaps the issue of vocabulary is something that we should discuss at a building-wide faculty meeting."

The team then continues to discuss other assessment items and to identify strategies to address each issue.

Ms. Shaw wraps up the meeting by saying, "Great job, everyone! Next time we will review the constructed-response and document-based-question sections. Remember to bring examples of your students' work for levels 1, 2, 3, and 4 on our common rubric. We can see from our data printout that our students did better on the writing sections than on the multiple choice, but we can always get better! Let's also plan to set our SMART goal for the next assessment. I'm seeing 90s in our future!"

The teachers in this story accomplished a great deal in a short time. Guided by the organizational skills of the teacher leader, the dialogue was on-task and targeted. Ms. Shaw came to the meeting prepared with a focused agenda. She also supplied pertinent data: an item analysis that showed student responses for each possible answer in the multiple-choice section. Teachers were easily able to determine which questions caused the most difficulty and which were correctly answered by most of the students. Clearly, this team had developed a routine—a flow. Risk-free support and a focus on strengthening the grade-level program to promote student achievement were clear.

But do team meetings flow this seamlessly every day? Realistically, there are always bumps along the road to collaboration. Take, for example, the teacher who has a particularly challenging class. She may use the same read-aloud story and extension task that the team agrees to add to the curriculum. But when reviewing student work at a subsequent meeting, she finds that her students achieved well below her teammates' classes. What to do?

It is important for the team leader to reinforce that data are not used to judge but rather serve as a guide to learning for the entire team. In this risk-free environment, the team members can comfortably discuss how they delivered their lessons. The team leader might ask a variety of guiding questions to direct the dialogue. How did each teacher on the team differentiate the assignment to meet student needs? What strategies were used during the read-aloud? Might the team want to mix students from all classrooms from time to time to differentiate delivery? Might our frustrated teacher be able to pick up some new ideas by observing a teammate who has a strength in using literacy strategies? It is important to remember that each team member brings strengths to the total team. Today's frustrated teacher may deliver tomorrow's success story. There are numerous possible solutions. DuFour, DuFour, Eaker, and Many (2006, p. 107) reinforce that a collaborative "group-think" brings more viable approaches to the table than leaving teachers isolated to ponder on their own:

> The very reason any organization is established is to bring people together in an organized way to achieve a collective purpose that cannot be accomplished by working alone....The degree to which people are working together in a coordinated, focused effort is a major determinant of the effectiveness of any organization.

Through collaboration, a school or district can tap the expertise of all members in support of the common mission, vision, values, and goals that drive their entire PLC forward.

Teacher Leaders as Lifelong Learners

In summary, all of a PLC's teacher leaders must exemplify the vision of lifelong learning. If the universal focus of mission statements is to support lifelong learning, then all educators must be committed to putting that mission into action in their own lives. They must model the value of continuous learning if they are to espouse that goal for their students. In the words of Roland Barth,

> Just as potters cannot teach others to craft in clay without setting their own hands to work at the wheel, so teachers cannot fully teach others the excitement, the difficulty, the patience, and the satisfaction that accompany learning without themselves engaging in the messy, frustrating, and rewarding "clay" of learning. (1990, p. 49)

It is through colleague-to-colleague support that a professional learning community grows. Teacher leaders are the change agents, the facilitators of learning in a PLC. Whether offering a strategy that works in their classrooms during a team meeting, modeling for colleagues in the classroom setting, facilitating a workshop session, or serving as mentors, teachers teaching teachers is a powerful model for promoting differentiated job-embedded professional development. As DuFour, DuFour, and Eaker propose in *Revisiting Professional Learning Communities at Work*, "it is time to embrace a new story, a new image of teaching, one that celebrates professionals who work together interdependently to accomplish collectively what they could never accomplish alone" (2008, p. 182). By pooling individual strengths, the collective whole is strengthened to provide optimum support for student and adult learning.

CHAPTER 8

Time Out!

"So much to do, so little time." This lament is often heard as teachers face the growing need for ongoing professional learning to address current research and best practice, high-stakes testing and ever-changing educational mandates. As the needs of districts increase and budgets decrease, the opportunities for paid summer or after-hours work evaporate, leaving educators to support their growth as a learning community within the confines of the work-day. How can districts balance the need for professional development with the need to keep teachers in their classrooms with their students? How can they find the time to implement the strategies for differentiated professional learning that we have discussed in the previous chapters of this book? How can they shape the workday to provide the necessary time for collaboration and ongoing learning? It is imperative to find a solution, because "leaders cannot accept scarcity of time as justification for not moving forward" (DuFour et al., 2006, p. 195).

The answer lies in a belief in the power of job-embedded professional development. The time dilemma provides districts with the opportunity to put this belief into practice. We propose that professional development will produce desired effects only if the total school community embraces it. It is when professional development is fed to teachers in small bites that they willingly come to the table.

Christine Lowden (2006) finds that effective professional development is tied to districts' goals and consists of inquiry, action research, reflection, collaboration, and mentoring. In this chapter, we will share several models that create time for targeted professional development opportunities that incorporate maximum initial learning followed by support, practice, mentoring, and reflection. Conference days, early release or late arrival days, and roll-through sessions optimize time out for collaboration and systemic professional growth. In-house colleague-to-colleague support provides the glue to strengthen the learning between sessions.

Superintendent's Conference Day Time

Nearly every district in the country schedules superintendent's conference days. Frequently, these consist of "sit and get" workshops where well-known speakers present motivating speeches to large multi-district audiences to help educators celebrate the importance of their role in creating the leaders of tomorrow. Sometimes districts offer more targeted workshops presented by experts who share their knowledge on a given topic and then fly off to their next engagement, never to be heard from again. Certainly these presentations have their place when they are designed to reinforce or expand a staff's shared knowledge on a vital topic or are used to introduce all staff members to an important concept. But to optimize their impact, district and school leaders must choose one-day events that connect to teachers' needs, and they must provide a variety of follow-up opportunities to reinforce and embed the new learning.

That said, changing the traditional focus of conference days is a good way to provide additional time for job-embedded professional development and colleague-to-colleague collaboration. We recommend that the *majority* of conference days be devoted to work that furthers the targeted goals of vertical, departmental, and grade-level teams. As discussed in the previous chapter, teams facilitated by teacher leaders provide the structure for working on curriculum alignment, analyzing data, and refining common local assessments. A school's or district's teams may be at varying stages of addressing the four guiding questions formulated by DuFour et al. (2008, pp. 183–84):

1. What is it that we want our students to learn? What knowledge, skills and dispositions do we expect them to acquire as a result of this course, grade level, or unit of instruction?

2. How will we know if each student is learning each
    of the essential skills, concepts, and dispositions
    we have deemed most essential?

3. How will we respond when some of our students
    do not learn? What process will we put in place
    to ensure students receive additional time and
    support in a timely, directive, and systematic way?

4. How will we enrich and extend the learning for
    students who are already proficient?

Team learning, targeted professional development, and collegial support enable the effective implementation of interventions for struggling students and enrichment for the highfliers.

Early Release and Late Arrival Time

The time provided by infrequent superintendent's conference days is typically not sufficient to meet a district's professional development needs. Another vehicle for creating time for collaboration and adult learning is the early release day (ERD) or late arrival day (LAD). For an ERD, students are released two to three hours earlier than the regular dismissal to allow time for professional development. Similarly, for an LAD, the students' school day starts at a later time on the given date. The number of such days may vary from state to state, depending on student attendance regulations. Typically, two or three ERDs or LADs per semester are acceptable to the community, parents, and staff. Understandably, districts struggle with student release time versus instructional time but realize the necessity of giving their staffs time for collaboration in order to guarantee the most effective program for students. ERDs and LADs provide an opportunity for collaborative teams to continue work on targeted goals or to build common knowledge on an identified topic that will be incorporated into grade-level or departmental work. For example, teams might attend data workshops focused on the results of state or local common assessments, math problem-solving workshops presented by math lead teachers, and document-based-question workshops for social studies and ELA teachers. Topics would be dependent on each school's or district's data-driven targets and the needs of subsets of teachers who may or may not have the same needs as the school or district.

But what can districts do beyond the release time/arrival time model? How can they provide additional time for teacher learning as well as for collaboration?

Roll-Through Time

The roll-through is a unique and exciting vehicle for delivering short, targeted professional development to teachers without significant disruption of classroom instruction. A roll-through brings specific groups of staff members together for identified learning followed by individualized, differentiated coaching in the classroom. Teachers then return to the table to reflect, share, and extend their learning at the next roll-through. This model provides the opportunity to involve the entire school community in action research and collaboration.

An efficient roll-through requires hiring enough substitutes to cover one grade level or department at a time. These substitute teachers cover classes long enough (usually one to two hours) for the regular teachers to participate in the learning session. Substitutes then "roll" to the classrooms of the next grade level or department, enabling all teachers from all grades or departments to engage in professional development in small groups. It is possible to offer targeted sessions to an entire building in one or two days, with time for the discussion, modeling, guided practice, and questions necessary for achieving desired results. Teachers are taken away from their students for only a few hours at a time rather than a few days at a time. The roll-through model is used again when teachers attend follow-up sessions for reflection and sharing. A roll-through provides the time both to address specific issues of importance to a grade or department and to meet individual needs. The richness comes after each roll-through, as teachers and in-house facilitators work together in classrooms to embed the new learning with their students.

Table 8.1 shows a possible roll-through schedule for a K–5 elementary school. This schedule allows for all six grade levels to meet with only one and a half days of substitute time. The building must hire enough substitutes to cover the largest grade level. For smaller grade levels, with prior planning, the additional substitutes can provide small-group support for targeted student needs while waiting to cover the next roll-through for the regular staff.

Table 8.1: Sample Elementary Roll-Through Schedule

Time	Grade Level or Activity
Day 1	
8:00–9:15	Kindergarten
9:30–10:45	Grade 1
11:00–12:15	Grade 2
12:15–1:15	Lunch
1:15–2:30	Grade 3
2:30–3:30	Facilitators debrief and prepare for Day 2
Day 2	
8:00–9:15	Grade 4
9:30–10:45	Grade 5
10:45–12:15	Facilitators debrief

Table 8.2 shows a possible schedule for a secondary roll-through.

Table 8.2: Sample Secondary Roll-Through Schedule

Time	Department or Activity
8:00–9:15	English
9:30–10:45	Social studies
11:00–12:15	Science
12:15–1:15	Lunch
1:15–2:30	Math
2:30–3:30	Debrief

Both sample schedules are based on a model in which in-house professional developers are presenting workshops and must be provided with time for lunch and debriefing. (In cases where grade levels or departments are participating in team collaboration time with a lead teacher facilitator, additional roll-through time is available, since the lead teacher would be meeting only with his or her team and would not need the additional time to eat or debrief that is necessary when professional developers are meeting with several teams.) Staggering the lunch periods for substitutes to match periods when fewer teachers are attending learning sessions increases the number of possible roll-throughs per day.

Let's take a look at an example. One district's elementary math instructional support teachers (ISTs) saw the roll-through as the ideal vehicle for introducing the entire elementary staff to a common math problem-solving model. In the first year of the Math Problem-Solving Initiative, teachers attended a roll-through with their grade-level colleagues nearly every month. At each session, they were introduced to a problem-solving strategy based on the work of noted math researchers Marilyn Burns and Sue O'Connell. Teachers engaged in guided practice using an adult math problem and then were given several lessons with grade-level problems to take back to their classrooms.

After the initial strategy roll-through, the ISTs scheduled push-in lessons with each grade-level teacher and special educator to model the use of the strategy with groups of students. Teachers then spent time teaching additional lessons that the ISTs gave them to practice and support the newly learned strategy. During the next roll-through, teachers debriefed and shared their successes and challenges. As a collaborative team, they shared student work, modified existing lessons, and explored new thinking. This accomplished, the next strategy was introduced and modeled, and teachers were sent off to practice once again. The roll-through made it possible for teachers to embed nine new math problem-solving strategies into their daily practice in one year of professional development.

In the following years, the number of roll-through sessions decreased while classroom support was augmented and differentiated to meet individual teacher needs. Currently, modeling is still offered, as well as co-teaching and peer-to-peer observation and support. Teacher trainers continue to facilitate roll-through sessions to address instructional gaps identified through the ongoing analysis of student assessment data.

The beauty of the roll-through is that teachers can meet and learn together in short blocks of time and then return to their classrooms to refine and solidify new practices. These opportunities for incremental, targeted professional development are a productive and cost-effective model for finding time within the workday with minimal impact on classroom instruction.

Release Time

In order to promote key initiatives, it is also necessary to give staff members release time and to provide substitutes so that they can attend occasional full-day or half-day workshops. Once again, any conference or workshop that takes a teacher away from the classroom must be directly aligned with the professional learning community's mission, vision, goals, and data-driven targets or must augment teachers' content knowledge with a direct connection to the established curriculum. Sending one or two teachers to attend a conference based strictly on teacher interest will not move a PLC forward. If a district is sending teacher leaders to bring back new knowledge to augment in-house expertise, conference attendance is valid. If a district has established a series of workshops to support new teachers or to build a stronger base of common understanding of a topic that directly supports a goal, that is also valid. However, the rationale of "that sounds like an interesting conference" might not be supported unless there is a direct connection to the curriculum, teachers' pedagogical needs, or other areas that will have a positive impact on student learning.

The challenge of appropriately using release time for conferences also ties into the availability of opportunities for follow-up and reflection. Even the most engaging conference will produce nothing more than a binder collecting dust on a shelf if new learning is not applied and reinforced. "Use it or lose it" could not be truer! Once again, the alignment with mission, vision, values, and goals, combined with a means to embed the new learning within the existing structure, is essential.

Restructuring the Workday

In addition to providing the occasional scheduled opportunities for collaboration and professional learning that we have been discussing, districts are challenged with finding the means to include colleague-to-colleague planning and collaborative team meetings in each teacher's regular schedule. We embrace the National Staff Development Council's credo, found on their website and throughout their publications: "Every educator engages in effective professional learning every day so every student achieves" (2009b, homepage). Stephanie Hirsh and Joellen Killion share their vision that "in the next decade, we want conversations to begin with the question of how to restructure the school year and day so that learning with colleagues is a mandatory part of every workday for every educator" (2007, p. 110). We would argue that we do not need to wait. By casting aside restrictions imposed by master schedules that may be entrenched in "the way we have always done it," creative scheduling can provide opportunities for teachers to meet regularly to plan and to learn collaboratively within their workday. As shown in previous chapters, the power of colleague-to-colleague support is unsurpassed in enhancing adult learning. Time must and can be provided. Simply put, we must constantly be on the lookout for creative ways to find time within the workday for teacher learning and collaboration.

One solution at the elementary level is to devise a building schedule that provides each grade level with a common period free of student supervision. This can be achieved through scheduling special-area courses at the same time for all students in a given grade level. Common student lunch and recess periods can also be used for this planning time. Teachers' individual preps and lunch periods can be staggered across the schedule; however, a minimum of one block of time per week should be arranged for grade-level collaboration.

It is also possible to create planning time at the secondary level. Schools can build master schedules that provide for collaboration time for all teachers who teach the same course. Itinerant teachers and singletons might develop email relationships with teachers from neighboring schools who teach the same course. Providing planning time for this "virtual team" can result in rich networking and creativity. At the middle school level, planning time for interdisciplinary teams has routinely been built into building schedules. Time for subject-area planning across the teams can also be arranged. For example, instead of scheduling grade-level interdisciplinary team meeting time each day, a school can use two or three of those days for collaboration within subject areas at the grade level while maintaining the remainder for interdisciplinary collaboration. Is it easy to do? Not always. Is it possible? Yes!

In addition to building in regularly scheduled time for collaboration, schools can be creative about uncovering other opportunities for planning and learning. For example, many elementary schools have a morning program, various assemblies throughout the year, activity fairs, and the like. Traditionally, all teachers are on deck to supervise. Do schools really need every teacher for the supervision of these schoolwide events? A rotating schedule can allow for some grade levels or departments to be released from supervision and to use the time for collaboration. Similar possibilities exist at the secondary level. Many middle and high schools have activity periods as part of their schedule. These time blocks give students opportunities for extracurricular activities and for extra help from teachers. Each day, teachers from a different department could be released to use this period for common planning time. We would caution, however, that the teacher-student relationship must be safeguarded. If the school has assigned students to specific teacher advisors, the activity period should be reserved for their regular one-on-one meetings.

Online Resources

Numerous online resources provide targeted professional development that teachers can access at their own convenience. We have already mentioned the power of connecting itinerant or singleton teachers to "virtual pen pals" in other districts. Online professional development programs can bring well-known researchers to a teacher's desktop. Such programs can strengthen a teacher's knowledge on a particular topic or can be used to bring teachers with common interests together. When a small group of teachers join together to watch an online presentation, the dialogue that is generated makes the experience all the more relevant. School-based discussions of online resources are similar to book talks, which continue to be a wonderful venue for professional growth. Webinars and other online chat groups can expand the dialogue outside the confines of a school building and provide for networking that is limitless. The possibilities are endlessly exciting. Providing time and structure to explore online resources is yet another way that a PLC can support and differentiate ongoing professional learning.

Harnessing Time

Shirley Hord and William Sommers (2008, page 109) affirm,

> Leaders must help create space for conversations to take place during the school day. We know that ongoing, job-embedded, and results-driven professional learning increases application of new ideas and practices with staff. Providing time to talk and reflect about our teaching profession is a critical link to sustaining ongoing learning in the organization.

Teachers realize that when they make a commitment to job-embedded professional development and find ways to use their workday time creatively, it is possible to help all students reach their academic and personal potential. They have discovered the power of collaboration and reflection. They feel energized with the immediacy of bringing new ideas from professional development sessions directly to the classroom. Persistence, thinking outside the box, and placing trust in their colleagues and administrators must guide learning communities in the efficient use of time for professional development.

CHAPTER 9

Ten Principles for Principals

Leading a learning community can entail a paradigm shift for a building principal. It provides an opportunity to be a transformational leader. In *School Leadership That Works*, Robert Marzano, Timothy Waters, and Brian McNulty (2005, p. 38) assert that "principals can have a profound effect on the achievement of students in their schools." Richard DuFour and Robert Eaker (1998) devote an entire chapter of their book *Professional Learning Communities at Work* to the role of the principal. DuFour, DuFour, and Eaker (2008) maintain that emphasis in *Revisiting Professional Learning Communities at Work*. The earlier book makes clear that "principals cannot transform a school through their individual efforts" yet points out that initiatives are unlikely to succeed "without effective leadership from the principal" (DuFour & Eaker, 1998, p. 203). In *The Principal as Staff Developer*, Richard DuFour asserts that "the principal is a key figure in determining the ultimate success of any effort to develop school personnel" (1991, p. 8).

For job-embedded differentiated professional development to take root, principals must not only understand the power of the model but also provide the necessary opportunities, structures, and resources for it to thrive. They must shape their days to allow time for these important aspects of leadership. They must be able to talk the talk and clearly walk that talk. When leadership professes to endorse the tenets of a collaborative culture yet still gives priority to managerial tasks, the proclamations and endorsements fall flat. As David Cottrell puts it in *Monday Morning Leadership*, the challenge is to "Keep the Main Thing the Main Thing" (2002, p. 27). For a professional learning community, learning must be the main thing.

Differentiated job-embedded professional development keeps it at the forefront.

Putting theory into practice can be an onerous task. The many fires that need attention on a given day are enough to overwhelm even the most competent and organized administrator. Given these challenges, how can a principal maintain a focus on learning? In this chapter, we offer ten principles that will guide principals in their efforts to support their teachers as they embed new learning into practice. We honor the fact that building administrators have many responsibilities but would offer that nurturing differentiated learning for students and staff must be a priority.

Revisiting Professional Learning Communities at Work advises principals of PLCs to define their job in the following terms: "My responsibility is to create the conditions that help the adults in this building continually improve upon their collective capacity to ensure all students acquire the knowledge, skills, and dispositions essential to their success" (DuFour et al., 2008, p. 309). Keeping a focus on adult learning is at the heart of the principal's work if all students are to reach their potential.

It is important that principals realize that the concept of differentiation in professional development does not mean that all teachers are "doing their own thing." Principals need to be well versed in the expectations of the district initiatives and the components of effective instruction. Then, through reflection on data, participation in collaborative team meetings, and classroom visitations, they can help target building-based professional development and guide each individual teacher to access the support needed for continuous improvement of pedagogical skills. This, in turn, will lead to increased student learning.

1. You Get What You Model

The principal must be the building's lead learner. "Do as I say, not as I do" will not work. To lead a true professional learning community, administrators must have a clear understanding of all professional development initiatives. No one is expecting the principal to be an expert in all areas; this is mission impossible. Teachers should expect, however, that their administrators have a working knowledge of the key components of all initiatives and that they understand the value of the "I Do, We Do, You Do" delivery model. If they don't, how are they going to ensure that best-practice instruction is being embedded in the classroom setting?

To this end, administrators must attend professional development sessions and be engaged in learning along with their staff on conference and release days. When workshops and roll-throughs are scheduled, attendance needs to be a priority on the principal's schedule. Principals must schedule time to attend collaborative team meetings. It is crucial to place these events *on the calendar* rather than hoping for the opportunity to "drop by." What gets scheduled gets done.

Obviously, this isn't easy. Emergencies arise, and principals are inundated with paperwork and crises. However, it is a rare day when it is *impossible* to spend time out of the office attending a workshop or team meeting or visiting a classroom to watch a strategy in action. How administrators spend their time reflects what they value. One cannot do *everything* in a given day, but one can do *anything* that is a priority. If principals expect teachers to prioritize continuous learning, to engage in action research, to collaborate in team meetings, and to model for their students, can they do any less as administrators? It is hypocritical to ask others to do something that one is unwilling to do oneself. We know a principal who schedules time each day to be in classrooms, attend team meetings, or do whatever is needed to be accessible to support the PLC. He does not leave these aspects of his job to chance. He makes them priorities.

When does an administrator find the time? Is it necessary to attend everything? Attending all professional development offerings may seem overwhelming, but being visible when teachers are engaged in learning shows the staff that the principal values what is being learned or discussed. For example, if teacher leaders are running a series of grade-level roll-throughs, the principal should pick one grade level to attend from start to finish, while dropping in on others.

The principal should switch the grade level that he or she attends each time.

Consider the practice of one building administrator who puts professional development dates on her monthly calendar *prior* to scheduling meetings and other obligations. She reserves time to attend every workshop, if not for the entire session then for long enough to engage in the key aspects of the learning and to validate the importance of the session by her presence.

If replicating this administrator's practice seems overwhelming, a principal could try creating a schedule to ensure that one member of the administrative team would attend each session. The duties should be shared so that at least one administrator is available. The bottom line is to regard professional learning as a priority, not to leave it at the mercy of one's daily schedule. It should not be an extra to fit in if there is nothing else to do, but rather a vital component of one's role as a learning leader.

If principals' district or building cultures make it impossible to attend in-house trainings in their entirety, they should consider developing mini-courses for their administrative teams. For example, they could schedule a series of after-school sessions designed to give administrators an understanding of current initiatives, including key elements to look for when observing a lesson and significant questions to ask in pre- and post-teacher conferences. When teachers are aware of these sessions, they will honor the fact that the district is also differentiating professional development for administrators. Thus, when principals drop by the learning sessions instead of attending them in their entirety, staff members will realize that this does not mean that they do not have the training and knowledge necessary to move the initiative forward, but rather have approached their own learning in a way that better meets their needs.

2. Data and Evidence Define Focus

Principals need to value the importance of data in driving instruction, both in the classroom and in the building as a whole. Administrators and teachers should collaborate in reviewing data, not only from state accountability assessments but also from common local assessments. Teacher leaders can carry out the time-consuming mining of data, but the principal must be aware of trends in order to help validate and support the professional development needed to close any gaps in student achievement. Jeff Nelson, Joe Palumbo, Amalia Cudeiro, and Jan Leight (2005, p. 20) speak to the importance of determining a building's "instructional focus ... based on every student's learning needs as evidenced by multiple sources of data." In our work we often marry the concepts of "data" and "evidence." Taking a hard look at statistical data is important, yet it is equally important to look at the "soft" data that come from observations, discussions, and analyses of student work to see how well strategies are being embedded in students' practice. Both statistical and anecdotal data are important.

To support differentiation in professional development, principals should ask teachers to identify their own areas of strength and areas for growth, based on assessments of their students' work. The point of principals' gathering and reviewing data is not to be threatening or evaluative, but rather to help provide the support that is most relevant to each teacher. Just as data help determine district- and schoolwide goals, as well as interventions for individual students, when the principal and teacher review classroom data and observation reports together, they can decide on what professional development will best fit the teacher's needs. Once a focus area is determined, it gives direction to the instructional support teachers, literacy leaders, mentors, and others as they support the classroom teacher.

The principal is also responsible for making all relevant data available to the building's departmental and grade-level learning teams and requiring that their decision making be data driven. As these teams review their collective data and evidence of best practices, they set goals for their students and for their own learning. Taken one step further, the big-picture items become the building's goals.

One district in our region schedules "data huddles" after each assessment, during which teachers have time to review and analyze student achievement data. They celebrate their areas of strength and target those areas that need additional support. This is an example of the "learning by doing" that is characteristic of high-functioning PLCs. DuFour et al. (2006, p. 207) describe the power of this process: "When educators learn to clarify their priorities, to assess the current reality of their situation, to work together, and to build continuous improvement into the very fabric of their collective work, they create conditions for the ongoing learning and self-efficacy essential to solving whatever problems they confront."

3. Empower Teacher Leaders

The best professional developers are those closest to the action. The expertise within the walls of every school is phenomenal! As Mike Schmoker (2006, p. 118) states, "Internal expertise is of more value than what we import." Terri Martin (2008, p. 147) reinforces this theme when she observes that "it is time to stop looking outside for what will fix our schools and know that it is what we already have inside that counts."

As the previous chapters have shown, colleague-to-colleague support must be a component of all that we do. No one person can move a school forward; many hands and minds must pave the way to greater student achievement. During a question/answer session after Stephen Covey delivered the keynote address at the 2008 meeting of the National Staff Development Council, a participant asked him to define leadership. He replied that "leadership is communicating people's worth and potential so clearly that they are inspired to see it in themselves." By valuing and harnessing the energy and expertise of teacher leaders at the building level, the principal empowers the entire PLC and expands the potential for supporting differentiated professional development. In the previous chapters, we described how lead teachers, instructional support teachers, literacy specialists, and mentors can be used to set professional development agendas, provide workshop sessions, and, through coaching, support their colleagues with ongoing feedback. Teachers know what they need to learn, and they also know who the experts are among them. Every classroom teacher is motivated when his or her expertise is recognized and valued.

The principal's role is to mentor these teacher leaders, give them support, be sure they have the necessary resources, and, most of all, be their main cheerleader along the journey. Should the PLC encounter blockers, principals can serve as buffers for any staff pushback. Principals need to clearly reinforce that teacher leaders do not evaluate other teachers but serve as a resource to provide support.

We can see how vital a role principals play when we realize the impact that the pioneers, settlers, and outlaws can exert on a professional learning community. Principals must validate and support the pioneers as they chart their data-driven course and begin their exploration. The pioneers may periodically seek guidance from their principals as they continue along their journey. Once the pioneers have established protocols, completed action research, and achieved success, principals should encourage the settlers to join them. As the pioneers guide the settlers, the school culture begins to change, with the majority of teachers implementing the new learning. Principals must make it clear that, although they are open to constructive input and will listen to data-driven suggestions from all, they will not allow the outlaws to sabotage the work that has been successfully accomplished. They must clearly reaffirm the purpose of the cultural change and provide the professional development necessary to convince the outlaws to join their colleagues. However, if the outlaws continue to take potshots at the settlement (the embedded district initiatives), the principal must ultimately have the tenacity to encourage them to find another settlement where they may find more professional comfort. The climate of a PLC may not be the right fit for all.

Throughout their research on and writing about professional learning communities, DuFour, DuFour, Eaker, and Many speak to the importance of *simultaneous loose and tight leadership*. They define this leadership style as one "in which leaders encourage autonomy and creativity (loose) within well-defined parameters and priorities (tight)" (2006, p. 218). The relationship between teacher leaders and principals as they support differentiated professional development in their PLC is an example of this loose/tight model. Principals can be "loose" by empowering teacher leaders to share their collective knowledge through collaboration and coaching; at the same time, they can be "tight" about sticking to the targeted data- and evidence-driven priorities that have been established.

Let's look at an example of this simultaneous loose and tight leadership in action. A literacy specialist wants to offer the math department a roll-through on writing in the content area and is meeting with the principal to introduce his proposal. The principal asks, "What data support your selection of this focus for the next roll-through schedule?" The literacy specialist shares data from the recent state assessment that the math teachers reviewed in their last collaborative team meeting. The teachers had examined their students' tests to identify the most common area of weakness. In the extended-response sections that required students to explain their work, many students had been unable to articulate how they had arrived at their answers. Upon reflection, the teachers realized that they had been stressing computation but had not given their students adequate time to practice writing. Furthermore, the teachers decided that they needed professional development in how to teach writing in their content area. As math teachers, they wanted to learn how to teach and model effective writing strategies to address the identified need and increase their students' achievement.

This conversation satisfies the need for tight leadership. The principal can be confident that the focus for the professional development is data driven and that collaboration with the literacy specialist will support the math department's goals for increasing student achievement. Now the principal can be loose and give the literacy specialist total autonomy to design the learning session and to provide follow-up support for the math teachers. The principal will attend the roll-through in order to reinforce the cycle of job-embedded support.

4. Foster a Safe Environment

Pioneering must be encouraged. This principle goes hand in hand with the need to empower teacher leaders. When teachers want to try something new that is grounded in best-practice research and supported by student achievement data, they must be encouraged to take that risk.

Changing a culture takes time. A safe environment is not established overnight. It takes more than rhetoric. When teachers see that there is no risk of negative repercussions, they will feel increasingly comfortable to try new things, to be monitored along the way, and to make adjustments as necessary. This should not be misconstrued to mean that principals should encourage teachers to jump on every "flavor of the month." Not at all! What it means is that teachers need to feel supported as they take on the role of learner, practice the strategies that they have learned in professional development, and move out of their comfort levels to try something that is new to them. Teachers need to feel safe to seek guidance from their principals, to say that they need support, and to be honest with their fellow team members about their individual needs for growth. Principals must be nonjudgmental and willing to differentiate the kinds of support they offer in response to teachers' expressed needs. Often teachers need to be given time: for practice, for more demonstrations by teacher leaders, for more team reflection. Often they need empathic listening and constructive suggestions.

Principals, too, need to feel safe to express their own needs for professional development. When teachers see administrators engage in their own professional learning, it is a clear validation of the importance of continuous growth and learning for all. Once again, it comes down to walking the talk. In *Leading Professional Learning Communities*, Shirley Hord and William Sommers (2008, p. 29) stress that "when the principal and staff members focus on their own learning, together they begin to develop ways to make learning happen. It is not enough to say that we believe in staff learning; we have to demonstrate that by meeting, learning together, sharing knowledge and skills." As we learn and grow together, the collective strength of our professional learning community is enhanced, and our students are the beneficiaries.

How does a principal model this risk taking? One way is to participate alongside teachers in a professional development workshop. Instead of sitting in the back of the room as an observer or making the occasional drop-by visit, a principal can literally come to the table as a participant, engaging in the workshop with teacher colleagues. This requires the principal to attend sessions in their entirety, to do the homework, and to participate in the activities as part of the group. When an administrator is open to asking questions and engaging as a learner, teachers realize that he or she is a lifelong learner too. When a principal exhibits curiosity about a topic and an openness to learning, his or her relationships to teachers as fellow educators become more authentic.

Another way to establish a readiness to learn is to solicit the input of the building's teacher leaders. By valuing the expertise of staff and truly participating in the collaborative environment, the principal walks the talk of the PLC. Principals should be willing to seek information and to acknowledge where they need to learn. In short, they should embrace the need to differentiate their own professional learning paths. They should be *learning leaders*.

5. Build Bridges Between Grade Levels and Schools

One of the biggest struggles in most school districts is the articulation of curriculum and instruction between grade levels and buildings. How much time is wasted on reteaching, simply because teachers are not cognizant of the curricula that come before and after their own grade levels? It is the role of the principal to ensure that time is allotted for conversations between grade levels and between buildings. Just as teachers must come out of their classrooms and collaborate within their grade level and building, so too must administrators share their expertise districtwide as they pursue an aligned K–12 professional development program for all teachers.

When principals model the power of colleague-to-colleague sharing by taking the time to visit their administrative colleagues in buildings across the district, they strengthen their knowledge of systemic practices. For example, if elementary principals were to occasionally "job swap" with their middle school counterparts, they would be able to experience middle school classrooms and team meetings firsthand. The middle school principals would likewise be connected with the building cultures that precede the middle level. What a wealth of understanding this would produce at both levels! Principals of middle and high schools could also adopt the job-swapping practice.

With the reality of time demands, colleague-to-colleague visits may not be feasible as often as principals might like. To continue the bridge building beyond the visits, districts should use their regular district-level administrative meetings to highlight happenings, successes, and challenges in each school. Enabling a district's learning leaders to develop a systemic understanding enhances the embedding of districtwide professional development and helps to support the differentiated needs of buildings, grade levels, and individual teachers.

6. Support the Big Picture of Systemic Initiatives

Directly related to the bridging between grade levels and buildings is the support of district initiatives. Principals need to know the key elements of district initiatives at all grade levels throughout the district. Once again, it is not expected that principals be experts in all areas, but a working knowledge of expectations and priorities is essential in creating a seamless K–12 program.

Instead of spending all of their administrative meeting time on managerial tasks, districts can use the traditional central office/building administrators' meetings as an opportunity to walk the talk of a collaborative culture with a focus on learning. Following the same model as the teachers' collaborative teams, the administrative team becomes a vehicle for professional growth. The PLC leaders engage in collective inquiry, study student achievement data, and continuously build their shared knowledge through book talks that help to define their roles as lead learners. They live the process along with their teacher teams. In this way, the continuity of a district's vision and beliefs is strengthened. Because of this shared purpose, when it is time to allocate funds, it is more likely that one school will sacrifice in order to support a program at another school that is essential for the flow of the district initiatives.

7. Allocate Resources to Support Professional Learning

We all know the saying "Put your money where your mouth is." This is another example of the need to walk the talk. In conjunction with their district office colleagues, principals must provide the resources necessary to support differentiated professional growth. Often, time is the key resource (see chapter 8). Teachers need time to review data and to collaborate. When teachers also have opportunities for colleague-to-colleague visits and for coaching support in the classroom, this is the most powerful form of professional development. But without the necessary funding, it will not happen. The teacher leaders can move the staff forward; the principal must provide the resources. Creating professional libraries, equipping workshop sessions with the necessary books and supplies, and, once again and most importantly, providing time all have a budgetary impact. Principals must keep differentiated professional development in mind when creating building budgets.

In times of budget cuts and fiscal challenges, the priorities of a PLC are put to the test. Professional development cannot be the sacrificial lamb. Although desperate times may call for desperate measures, reductions in professional development should be commensurate with cuts in other areas. Opportunities for collaboration and learning may be modified, and "outside of the box" options may be needed. However, modeling that learning continues to be the "main thing" becomes all the more important. When districts strike first at their professional development, they are striking at the heart of their existence, cutting off their lifeblood.

When our schools are challenged by budget woes at both the federal and state levels, how can we continue to fund the needed differentiated job-embedded professional development? Maximizing the role of in-house professional development in lieu of spending money on outside resources is a financially viable means of reducing overall expenditures while continuing to prioritize ongoing adult learning. We have already explored ways to "find" time within the workday for collaboration and professional development. The roll-through is a time-efficient and cost-effective delivery model. Title I funds can promote literacy learning across the grade levels. Title IIA and D funding can be targeted to support learning opportunities. Creativity within the negotiation process is another possible avenue. Districts cannot do everything that they have done in the past, but they can typically do anything that is a priority.

8. Be Visible

The paperwork that plagues all administrators can be over-whelming. Email itself has become the nemesis of time management. However, excuses aside, the principal must be in classrooms, infor-mally watching "We Do" collaboration and the resulting "You Do" learning in action. Nelson et al. (2005) propose that principals spend 50 percent of their time in classrooms. That would be marvelous and a goal to reach for. However, recognizing all of the demands on a principal's time, we would simply underscore the need to make this a scheduled priority that is part of regular practice.

Principals need to have ongoing conversations with teachers concerning how they are infusing professional development initia-tives into their daily instruction. According to Hord and Sommers (2008, p. 104), "Without substantive conversations about real class-room practice, not much transfer, reflection, or application to teach-ing practice will occur." If the focus for the elementary unit is on math problem-solving, principals should make a point of dropping by classrooms during math time. If the secondary buildings are tar-geting reading in the content areas, this should be on the principal's radar screen as he or she visits classrooms.

When principals observe teachers using best-practice strategies, it is important for them to provide positive reinforcement by letting the teachers know how much they value their willingness to learn through differentiated, job-embedded support. One building admin-istrator leaves positive sticky notes for teachers when he exits a class-room. It takes only a moment, but it works miracles. Do we ever get too old to appreciate being acknowledged for our achievements? Perhaps these notes wind up on the teachers' refrigerator doors.

Commenting on teachers' strategies also demonstrates that the principal is acutely aware of what teachers are learning in professional development and using in the classroom. On the flip side, watching teachers in action helps the principal to identify areas for improvement. In short, this should be a regular process, not one reserved solely for formal observation days.

9. Plan Faculty Meetings to Promote Learning

Often the mention of a faculty meeting provokes a groan or a grimace, even from the most dedicated teachers. Principals are in control of whether teachers view these meetings as a necessary evil or as an opportunity to grow and learn together. With our current technology, we do not need to bring an entire staff together to make announcements. We have email. At the most, five or ten minutes should be devoted to those messages that one needs to be sure that everyone hears. Just as districts can change the focus of administrative meetings (as discussed under principle 6), so too can principals design faculty meetings to become avenues for collective learning.

Faculty meetings are a time for the principal to celebrate what is working as teachers embed best practices in their instruction. They are a time for teachers to share how differentiated professional learning has enhanced their teaching and how their use of new strategies has improved their students' learning. One principal we know reserves time on each faculty meeting agenda for this sharing of stories. Hearing success stories from their colleagues may motivate teachers to request peer visits or to ask for support from a teacher leader. When teachers talk about the ups and downs they have experienced in their action research, it helps to solidify the risk-free environment. It is another means of reinforcing the power of collaborative learning and differentiated professional development.

Jim LaPlant (1997, p. 54) states that "it becomes teachers' responsibility to create an environment conducive to student learning. Principals have responsibility for creating an environment conducive to teacher learning." Faculty meetings can serve as principals' "classrooms," where they can conduct follow-up mini-workshops that keep the professional development objectives on the front burner for all.

10. What Gets Assessed Gets Done

How often have we heard our students ask, "Is this going to be on the test?" They are checking to see if they will be held accountable, if the expected learning is important. Why would this change for adult learners?

Principals must reinforce district and building initiatives by making it clear to teachers that they are accountable for understanding and implementing them. When teachers attend a district literacy workshop, participate in data analysis, or share in team meetings, the principal should be asking to see lessons that illustrate what has been learned. Principals' observations and evaluations must focus on evidence of the embedding of initiatives.

Teacher leaders can do their very best to support their colleagues, but, as pointed out earlier, they do not (and should not) have an evaluative role. Once again, the principal's working knowledge of professional development is crucial. If learning is to be job embedded, it is the principal who will make the rubber meet the road. As teachers experience differentiated professional development, they become equipped to put learning into practice. The principal who enriches observations with dialogue to reinforce teacher learning provides many avenues for accountability.

The Principal as Learning Leader

In summary, it is the role of the principal to be a learning leader who keeps the staff on track in making learning the "main thing." Student learning is all-important, but student learning depends on teachers who are continuously learning. Data must drive instruction both for students and for staff. District initiatives that are research based and job embedded must be prioritized and reinforced at the building level. Teachers make the difference in the classroom; principals make the difference in providing a climate that ensures collaboration, program alignment, and the embedding of best practices in daily classroom instruction.

Leading a professional learning community is a cultural change for administrators, just as it is for teachers. It is not easy, but it is definitely doable. It is a question of priorities and time allotment. DuFour et al. (2008, p. 421) advise:

> It will always be easier to quit and return to the familiar than to persevere in the face of challenges, reversals, and disappointments. Therefore, the key to success in implementing PLC concepts is demonstrating the discipline to endure at the hard work of change rather than retreating to the comfort of traditional practices.

Differentiating professional development is indeed "hard work," but it is the key to unlocking learning for adults as well as students. When the learning leader engages in the process along with the teachers, models the attributes of a lifelong learner, and walks the talk of the professional learning community, students will reap the benefits.

CHAPTER **10**

Sharing the Journey

Our research and professional practice confirm that differentiated professional development works. Adults respond when there is a direct relationship between their learning and their students' achievement. The emotional, collegial connections that develop when colleagues support colleagues on the learning journey add richness to the learning process.

We hope that we have succeeded in our aim of giving readers the tools they need to implement a differentiated professional development model in their districts. Having seen that teachers on collaborative teams benefit from hearing their colleagues' stories of their own learning journeys, we would like to conclude by sharing the decadelong journey of our own district as it has embraced the challenges of becoming a professional learning community. Our story will trace those ten years through our personal lenses as mentor/ literacy specialist and administrator for the Maine-Endwell Central School District, located in the southern tier of New York State. We will describe the support strategies that have served as the foundation of our district's model and share the firsthand experiences that have cemented our professional convictions and resulted in writing this book. We will recount our district's celebrations and struggles.

Those readers whose districts have already embarked on the journey to becoming professional learning communities may be able to relate to our experiences and use them to address the challenges of a major cultural change. Those readers whose districts are contemplating a move to a PLC model may find that our story helps them avoid some bumps in the road. In either case, we hope that we will illuminate the impact of differentiating professional development to strengthen a learning community. In telling this story, we once again acknowledge the contributions of the numerous colleagues who walk the talk of a professional learning community and every stakeholder who is invested in making Maine-Endwell a lighthouse district.

The Evolution of Maine-Endwell

Located near the city of Binghamton, New York, Maine-Endwell combines the suburban community of Endwell and the rural town of Maine. It lies about an hour south of Syracuse and three hours northwest of New York City, near the Pennsylvania border. Locally referred to as M-E, the district is recognized for its strong academic program, with student achievement scores ranking at or near the top in the region. M-E's schools also make a strong showing when compared with similar schools across New York State. The district comprises two K–5 elementary schools, a 6–8 middle school, and a 9–12 high school. Its approximately 2,700 students are served by 530 staff members. Over half of the teachers have less than eight years' experience in teaching.

This book has presented the research base necessary to support a differentiated model of professional development. However, to make the model work, a collaborative professional learning community environment is essential. Maine-Endwell did not always offer such an environment. Our story of the developments that eventually allowed job-embedded professional development to take root and flourish takes us back to 1999. That year, Maine-Endwell experienced a transition in central office leadership that was pivotal. Prior to this time, direction was very top-down. For the most part, the four buildings functioned as individual units.

During the 1990s, Kathy was assistant principal at Maine-Endwell Middle School (MEMS). With the leadership of Principal Jack Touhey and the energy of the entire staff, MEMS had been engaged in a multiyear transformation from a traditional junior high school format to a middle school structure with six interdisciplinary teams. When Kathy looks back on her educational career, her years at MEMS were some of the most rewarding and challenging.

As Jack once observed, MEMS exhibited many of the basics of a professional learning community before we were introduced to the concept. Efforts to engage in collective learning, harness the expertise of teacher leaders, and support struggling students through a pyramid of interventions were in their early stages, not only at the middle school but also throughout the district. What was missing was a common district focus, a focus that would unite us as one district instead of four individual schools.

In July of 1999, Maine-Endwell appointed a new superintendent, Gary Worden. When Gary arrived, he pledged to create a flattened organization that would maximize the strengths of all stakeholders in a risk-free environment. Kathy, now the director of elementary education, worked with Gary to build trust and unite the district around a common purpose—to harness the skills of all staff members to support student achievement.

We can begin by sharing a story that illustrates the paradigm shift from isolation to the power of collaboration. In the summer of 1999, the elementary reading teachers and administrators met with Kathy to revisit and expand the goals of our K–5 literacy program. The team studied research, visited neighboring districts, and ultimately determined that we would pursue a balanced literacy approach based on the work of Fountas and Pinnell. We further decided that we wanted to bolster the knowledge base of our current reading teachers so that they could be the in-house trainers for their colleagues. Little did we know that this model was the seed for growing a job-embedded professional development model throughout the district! Once the research was completed and the decision made, we asked, "How will we support the professional development of our literacy teachers so that they can, in turn, serve as the facilitators for others?" One of our team members had heard of a literacy specialist in a neighboring district who was supporting students and staff in using the balanced literacy model. Her name was Linda Bowgren. Linda became our literacy consultant and facilitated our training of the trainers.

Over the course of the next two years, many events occurred that, in the proverbial 20/20 hindsight, provided the building blocks for a job-embedded professional development model. The October 1999 superintendent's conference day was devoted to "Building Bridges," as colleagues met in K–12 vertical teams to examine the successes and challenges for the four core areas of ELA, math, social studies, and science. Special-area teachers also met in districtwide vertical teams to accomplish this task. A commitment to the idea of teachers supporting teachers was taking root as colleagues discovered the power of their combined knowledge. In 2000, the district created thirty-four lead-teacher positions. Lead teachers continue to facilitate vertical/departmental team collaboration at their buildings and serve as liaisons with administrators and with their lead-teacher counterparts across the district. The lead-teacher positions have allowed the professional learning community at Maine-Endwell to flourish as differentiated team meetings are scheduled throughout the district to address the SMART goals of each team. Over the years, the bridges have grown stronger.

In the fall of 2000, Superintendent Gary Worden attended a conference where Rick DuFour gave the keynote address. Gary returned to M-E book in hand. He related what he had heard and invited the entire administrative team to read *Professional Learning Communities at Work.* "Read it, and you will recognize Maine-Endwell" was his message. As the excitement grew, a group of teachers and administrators traveled to Rochester, New York, to attend a workshop with Rick DuFour. His message, as Gary had promised, connected with the path that we were following. It validated our efforts and also pointed the way to more work that remained to be done. The energetic conversations in the two vehicles as we traveled back to Endwell converged on the same goal: we wanted to bring DuFour to M-E. Because of the DuFours' schedule, we would have to wait until October of 2003 for this event, but our work continued in full force.

During this time, Linda was fast at work building and supporting our literacy initiative. We launched a series of workshops for K–2 balanced literacy. In looking back, we realize that this was the birth of "I Do, We Do, You Do." Our literacy trainers presented a workshop to our primary teachers that introduced a philosophical base and began strategy building. Teachers returned to their class-rooms and practiced the new learning with their students. The read-ing teachers were on hand to support them. Teachers then attended the next workshop in the series, and the cycle continued. Our chal-lenge then, and one that still continues now, was to ensure that the gradual release of responsibility in the "We Do" and "You Do" phases did indeed lead to independent, embedded practice.

As the K–2 initiative strengthened, our intermediate teachers asked, "When do we get our turn?" As a result, we developed a cadre of facilitators for grades 3–8. Now teachers in both the elementary and middle schools could join together for research-based literacy workshops geared to their grade levels and delivered using the same model of demonstrations followed by coaching and reflection. The high school teachers would soon follow suit. Workshops for reading and writing in the content areas were launched, and a K–12 con-tinuum was complete.

How did Kathy's role as director of elementary education evolve to meet the challenges of the learning community culture? The origi-nal director's role was similar to that of a professional developer. The two directors (one elementary and one secondary) would plan, orga-nize, and often deliver the professional development for conference days. Most professional development was in a large-group setting using a one-size-fits-all model. It needed to be that way. Who else would "stand and deliver"? But with the advent of a learning commu-nity and the emerging role of teacher leaders, the focus of professional development began to change. At this same time, Maine-Endwell was facing cuts in state funding. Our budget advisory team struggled with the realities of making cuts. Over the course of a few years, and in keeping with our belief in the power of teacher leadership, the district first chose to eliminate one director of instruction position in order to maintain the lead teacher positions and later eliminated both directorships. During that time, Kathy accepted the position of assistant superintendent for instruction, which absorbed the duties of the former directors' positions. Working as a facilitator, it was Kathy's role to bridge the K–12 district initiatives and support the evolving model of teacher-led professional development.

Another incident helps to illustrate Kathy's role in the evolution of Maine-Endwell's professional learning community. During the first year that she was director of elementary education, the elementary staff embarked on a search for social studies texts. A few years earlier, the district had adopted an elementary math text, and, in spite of the good intentions of all involved, the teachers felt that they had not been directly involved in the process. They lacked ownership and, in some cases, did not feel that the new text met the needs of the curriculum. We wanted to learn from experience and involve all stakeholders in making the next major purchase. The administrators and teacher leaders would select the viable options, and then all teachers would attend presentations and arrive at a common decision.

Realizing that the traditional formats for full- or half-day workshops would take up more time than necessary, Kathy experimented with a system for rotating substitutes between grade levels to allow every teacher to attend a presentation of approximately one hour with grade-level colleagues from both buildings. This was the birth of the roll-through that would come to be used throughout the district, as described in chapter 8.

In short, the role of district administrator evolved from a position of direct delivery to one of facilitator. Looking outside of the box and collaborating with stakeholders were key as we determined what was needed to move us forward and how support could be provided by and for those closest to the action.

October 2003 arrived, and the vision that was born in those two vehicles returning from Rochester three years earlier came to life. Both Rick and Becky DuFour addressed our K–12 community. Having the DuFours speak to our entire staff "up close and personal" was like going to the concert after loving the music for years. Once again, our efforts were validated and our challenges identified. Having all teachers and administrators hear the same message was a powerful experience that strengthened our foundation. Sharing common language and background knowledge helped our PLC leaders to solidify practices in our buildings and districtwide.

After the "big event," our journey continued. As each new PLC book came out, our teams read, reaffirmed, and advanced. We kept our strategies and objectives grounded in the four key questions posed by the DuFours, Eaker, and Many (2006, pp. 21, 46):

+ What is it we want our students to learn?

+ How will we know when each student has learned it?

+ How will we respond when some students do not learn?

+ How will we respond when some students have clearly achieved the intended outcomes?

In 2004, as mandated by the New York State Education Department, Maine-Endwell launched an official mentoring program for new teachers. A cross-district team of teachers and administrators worked with Kathy to research and develop a model. This team envisioned a two-pronged approach for supporting new teachers. First, we needed to hire a district-level mentor. Linda was ready for another professional challenge, and, as the saying goes, "the rest is history." Linda joined Maine-Endwell's Total Learning Community as our K–12 mentor. She soon recognized the importance of the second prong: professional development. The team developed a three-year job-embedded program to acculturate new teachers to our learning community. As the mentor, Linda infused the "I Do, We Do, You Do" model into her work. She also continued to be a key member of our literacy team, now serving as an in-house facilitator along with the colleagues whom she had trained. It is Linda's expertise as a professional developer that resounds throughout this book. As the induction program evolved, Kathy and Linda were able to work together on a regular basis. Kathy assumed the role of sounding board for Linda, becoming in effect the "mentor's mentor."

Reflecting on the Journey

Over the many months and years of our shared reading, research, and practice, our individual knowledge and perspectives have helped us arrive at our common belief in the power of differentiated professional development. We have supported each other's roles as we have blended the teacher and administrative perspectives to further teachers' learning and student achievement. It has been a journey of professional learning. We share a passion for teaching and learning and honor the impact that each teacher has on each student. Professional developers have a similar impact on adult learners. A fervent belief in the power of strengthening teacher performance by providing targeted, differentiated professional support will propel a professional learning community forward in support of student learning and achievement.

In closing, we want to emphasize that a successful differentiated professional development program is like any other effort—part research and planning and part people. The best plan in the world will falter if the people implementing it do not have a passion for the plan. The strength of our work lies in the strength of all of the teacher leaders and administrators who truly embrace the power of professional learning. Their stories join with ours and attest to the impact of Maine-Endwell's PLC. But the story isn't over: work remains to be done as the journey continues. The commonsense approach of differentiated job-embedded professional development will continue to support us as we learn and grow together.

We wish our readers well in their own journeys. If we can be of any further support, please feel free to contact us. We would be honored to try to differentiate our responses to meet your needs!

References and Resources

Bailey, S. (2004). Visual dialogue. In L. B. Easton (Ed.), *Powerful designs for professional learning* (pp. 245–56). Oxford, OH: National Staff Development Council.

Barker, K., Kagen, D., Klemp, R., Roderick, S., & Takenaga-Taga, D. (1997). *Toward a growth model of teacher professionalism.* Accessed at www.teachnet.org/TNPI/research/network/lafellows.htm on May 14, 2009.

Barth, R. (1990). *Improving schools from within.* San Francisco: Jossey-Bass.

Barth, R. (2006). Improving relationships within the schoolhouse. *Educational Leadership, 63* (6), 8–13.

Bowgren, L., & Sever, K. (2007). Shaping the workday. *Journal of Staff Development, 28*(2), 20–23.

Bowgren, L., & Sever, K. (2008). Shaping the workday. In V. von Frank (Ed.), *Finding time for professional learning* (pp. 125–28). Oxford, Ohio: National Staff Development Council.

Breaux, A., & Wong, H. (2003). *New teacher induction: How to train, support, and retain new teachers.* Mountain View, CA: Harry Wong Publications.

Burns, R. (2002). *The adult learner at work: The challenge of life-long education in the new millennium.* Crows Nest, N.S.W., Australia: Allen & Unwin.

Burns, S. (1995). Rapid changes require enhancement of adult learning. *HR Monthly*, June, 16–17.

Caldwell, S. (1997). *Professional development in learning-centered schools.* Topeka, KS: National Staff Development Council.

Cambourne, B. (1988). *The whole story: Natural learning and the acquisition of literacy in the classroom.* New York: Scholastic.

Cambourne, B. (1995). Toward an educationally relevant theory of literacy learning: Twenty years of inquiry. *Reading Teacher, 49,* 182–90.

Cambourne, B. (2002). The conditions of learning: Is learning natural? *Reading Teacher, 55*(8), 58–62.

Carlson, R., & Bailey, J. (1997). *Slowing down to the speed of life: How to create a more peaceful, simpler life from the inside out.* San Francisco: HarperCollins.

Conner, M. L. (1997–2004). Andragogy and pedagogy. *Ageless Learner.* Accessed at http://agelesslearner.com/intros/andragogy.html on May 14, 2009.

Cottrell, D. (2002). *Monday morning leadership.* Dallas, TX: Cornerstone Leadership Institute.

Covey, S. (1989). *The 7 habits of highly effective people.* New York: Free Press.

Danielson, C. (2006). *Teacher leadership that strengthens professional practice.* Alexandria, VA: Association for Supervision and Curriculum Development.

Darling-Hammond, L. (1997a). *Doing what matters most: Investing in quality teaching.* New York: National Commission on Teaching and America's Future.

Darling-Hammond, L. (1997b). *The right to learn: A blueprint for creating schools that work.* San Francisco: Jossey-Bass.

Diaz-Maggioli, G. (2004). *Teacher-centered professional development.* Alexandria, VA: Association for Supervision and Curriculum Development.

Drago-Severson, E. (2004). *Becoming adult learners: Principles and practices for effective development.* New York: Teachers College Press.

DuFour, R. (1991). *The principal as staff developer.* Bloomington, IN: National Educational Service.

DuFour, R., DuFour, R., & Eaker, R. (2008). *Revisiting professional learning communities at work: New insights for improving schools.* Bloomington, IN: Solution Tree.

DuFour, R., DuFour, R., Eaker, R., & Many, T. (2006). *Learning by doing: A handbook for professional learning communities at work.* Bloomington, IN: Solution Tree.

DuFour, R., & Eaker, R. (1998). *Professional learning communities at work: Best practices for enhancing student achievement.* Bloomington, IN: Solution Tree.

DuFour, R., Eaker, R., & DuFour, R. (2005). *On common ground: The power of professional learning communities.* Bloomington, IN: Solution Tree.

Eaker, R., DuFour, R., & DuFour, R. (2002). *Getting started: Reculturing schools to become professional learning communities.* Bloomington, IN: Solution Tree.

Feiman-Nemser, S., Carver, C., Schwille, S., & Yusko, B. (1999). Beyond support: Taking new teachers seriously as learners. In M. Scherer (Ed.), *A better beginning: Supporting and mentoring new teachers* (pp. 3–12). Alexandria, VA: Association for Supervision and Curriculum Development.

Fisher, D., & Frey, N. (2008). *Better learning through structured teaching: A framework for the gradual release of responsibility.* Alexandria, VA: Association for Supervision and Curriculum Development.

Fullan, M. (1993). *Change forces: Probing the depths of educational reform.* Bristol, PA: Falmer.

Fullan, M. (1997). Broadening the concept of teacher leadership. In S. Caldwell (Ed.), *Professional development in learning-centered schools* (pp. 34–48). Topeka, KS: National Staff Development Council.

Fullan, M. (2007). *The new meaning of educational change* (4th ed.). New York: Teachers College Press.

Fullan, M. (2008). *The six secrets of change.* San Francisco: Jossey-Bass.

Gallagher, K. (2003). *Reading reasons.* Portland, ME: Stenhouse.

Given, B. (2002). *Teaching to the brain's natural learning systems.* Alexandria, VA: Association for Supervision and Curriculum Development.

Glickman, C. D., Gordon, S. P., & Ross-Gordon, J. M. (2004). *Supervision and instructional leadership: A developmental approach.* Boston: Pearson.

Guskey, T. (2000). *Evaluating professional development.* Thousand Oaks, CA: Corwin.

Hall, G., & Loucks[-Horsley], S. (1979). *Implementing innovations in schools: A concerns-based approach.* Austin, TX: Research and Development Center for Teacher Education, University of Texas.

Hall, P., & Simeral, A. (2008). *Building teachers' capacity for success.* Alexandria, VA: Association for Supervision and Curriculum Development.

Heath, C., & Heath, D. (2007). *Made to stick.* New York: Random House.

Hernez-Broome, G., & Hughes, R. (2004). Leadership development: Past, present, and future. *Human Resources Planning, 27*(1), 24–32.

Hirsh, S., & Killion, J. (2007). *The learning educator: A new era for professional learning.* Oxford, OH: National Staff Development Council.

Holdaway, D. (2000). Affinities and contradictions: The dynamics of social or acquisition learning. *Literacy Teaching and Learning, 5*(1), 7–25.

Hord, S., Rutherford, W. L., Huling-Austin, L., & Hall, G. (1987). *Taking charge of change.* Alexandria, VA: Association for Supervision and Curriculum Development.

Hord, S. M., & Sommers, W. A. (2008). *Leading professional learning communities: Voices from research and practice.* Thousand Oaks, CA: Corwin.

Isaacs, W. (1999). *Dialogue and the art of thinking together.* New York: Doubleday.

Johnson, D. (2005). *Sustaining change in schools.* Alexandria, VA: Association for Supervision and Curriculum Development.

Joyce, B., & Showers, B. (2002). *Student achievement through staff development* (3rd ed.). Alexandria, VA: Association for Supervision and Curriculum Development.

Jung, C. G. (1974). *Psychological types* (Vol. 6). Bollingen Series. Princeton, NJ: Princeton University Press. (Original work published 1923)

Knight, J. (2007). *Instructional coaching: A partnership approach to improving instruction.* Thousand Oaks, CA: Corwin.

Knowles, M. S. (1975). *Self-directed learning: A guide for learners and teachers.* New York: Association.

Knowles, M. S. (1980). *The modern practice of adult education.* Chicago: Association/Follett.

Knowles, M. S. (1997). *The adult learner: A neglected species.* Houston, TX: Gulf Publishing. (Original work published 1973)

LaPlant, J. (1997). The principal's role and staff development. In S. Caldwell (Ed.), *Professional development in learning-centered schools* (pp. 50–62). Topeka, KS: National Staff Development Council.

Lent, R. C. (2006). *Engaging adolescent learners: A guide for content-area teachers.* Portsmouth, NH: Heinemann.

Lieb, S. (1991, Fall). Principles of adult learning. *Vision.* Accessed at http://honolulu.hawaii.edu/intranet/committees/FacDev Com/guidebk/teachtip/adults-2.htm on April 22, 2009.

Lindstrom, P., & Speck, M. (2004). *The principal as professional development leader.* Thousand Oaks, CA: Corwin.

Loughridge, M. E., Loughridge, M., & Tarantino, L. (2004). *Leading effective secondary school change: Your goal to strategies that work.* Thousand Oaks, CA: Corwin.

Lowden, C. (2006). Reality check. *Journal of Staff Development, 27* (1), 61–64.

Lyons, C. A., & Pinnell, G. S. (2001). *Systems for change in literacy education: A guide to professional development.* Portsmouth, NH: Heinemann.

Martin, Terri L. (2008). Professional learning in a professional learning community. In A. Buffum, C. Erkens, C. Hinman, S. Huff, L. G. Jessie, T. L. Martin, et al., *The collaborative administrator: Working together as a professional learning community* (pp. 143-57). Bloomington, IN: Solution Tree.

Marzano, R., Pickering, D., & Pollock, J. (2001). *Classroom instruction that works.* Alexandria, VA: Association for Supervision and Curriculum Development.

Marzano, R., Waters, T., & McNulty, B. (2005). *School leadership that works.* Alexandria, VA: Association for Supervision and Curriculum Development.

McDiarmid, G. W. (1995, April). *Realizing new learning for all students: A framework for the professional development of Kentucky teachers.* (NCRTL Special Report). East Lansing, MI: Michigan State University, National Center for Research on Teacher Learning.

McLaughlin, M. W. (1991). Enabling professional development: What have we learned? In A. Lieberman & L. Miller (Eds.), *Staff development for education in the '90s* (pp. 61–82). New York: Teachers College Press.

McNeil, P., & Klink, S. (2004). School coaching. In L. B. Easton (Ed.), *Powerful designs for professional learning* (pp. 175–84). Oxford, OH: National Staff Development Council.

McTighe, J. (2008). Making the most of professional learning communities. *Learning Principal, 3*(8), 1, 4–7.

Moller, G., & Pankake, A. (2006). *Lead with me: A principal's guide to teacher leadership.* Larchmont, NY: Eye on Education.

National Staff Development Council (2009a). *Definition of professional development.* Accessed at www.nsdc.org/standfor/definition.cfm on May 14, 2009.

National Staff Development Council. (2009b). *Our purpose.* Accessed at www.nsdc.org/standfor/definition.cfm on May 14, 2009.

Nelson, J., Palumbo, J., Cudeiro, A., & Leight, J. (2005). *The power of focus.* Huntington Beach, CA: Focus on Results.

Newmann, F. N. (1994, Spring). School-wide professional community. *Issues in Restructuring Schools, 6,* 1–2.

Pearson, P. D., & Gallagher, M. (1983). The instruction of reading comprehension. *Contemporary Educational Psychology, 8,* 317–44.

Podsen, I., & Denmark, V. (2000). *Coaching and mentoring first-year and student teachers.* Larchmont, NY: Eye on Education.

Reeves, D. (2008). *Reframing teacher leadership to improve your school.* Alexandria, VA: Association for Supervision and Curriculum Development.

Robb, L. (2000). *Redefining staff development: A collaborative model for teachers and administrators.* Portsmouth, NH: Heinemann.

Sachs, J. (1999, November). *Teacher professional identity: Competing discourses, competing outcomes.* Paper presented at AARE conference, Melbourne, Australia. Accessed at www.aare.edu.au/99pap/sac99611.htm on May 14, 2009.

Schlechty, P. (2005). *Creating the capacity to support innovations* (Occasional Paper #2). Louisville, KY: Schlechty Center for Leadership in School Reform.

Schmoker, M. (2006). *Results now.* Alexandria, VA: Association for Supervision and Curriculum Development.

Silver, H., Strong, R., & Perini, M. (1996). *Teaching styles and strategies: Interventions to enrich instructional decision-making* (3rd ed.). Woodbridge, NJ: Thoughtful Education.

Silver, H., Strong, R., & Perini, M. (2000). *So each may learn: Integrating learning styles and multiple intelligences.* Alexandria, VA: Association for Supervision and Curriculum Development.

Silver, H., Strong, R., & Perini, M. (2007). *The strategic teacher: Selecting the right research-based strategy for every lesson.* Alexandria, VA: Association for Supervision and Curriculum Development.

Silverstein, S. (1981). *A light in the attic.* New York: HarperCollins.

Smith, M. K. (2002). Malcolm Knowles, informal adult education, self-direction and andragogy. In *Encyclopedia of informal education.* Accessed at www.infed.org/thinkers/et-knowl.htm on May 15, 2009.

Sparks, D. (2005). *Leading for results.* Thousand Oaks, CA: Corwin.

Sparks, D., & Loucks-Horsley, S. (1989). Five models for staff development for teachers. *Journal of Staff Development, 10*(4), 40–57.

Speck, M., & Knipe, C. (2005). *Why can't we get it right? Designing high-quality professional development for standards-based schools.* Thousand Oaks, CA: Corwin.

Sweeny, B. (2003). *The CBAM: A model of the people development process*. Accessed at www.mentoring-association.org/membersonly/CBAM.html on March 28, 2009.

Tomlinson, C. A. (1995). *Differentiating instruction for advanced learners in a mixed-ability middle school classroom.* (ERIC Document Reproduction Service No. ED389141)

Tomlinson, C. A. (1999). *The differentiated classroom: Responding to the needs of all learners.* Alexandria, VA: Association for Supervision and Curriculum Development.

Tomlinson, C. A. (2001). *How to differentiate instruction in mixed-ability classrooms* (2nd ed.). Alexandria, VA: Association for Supervision and Curriculum Development.

Tomlinson, C. A. (2003). *Fulfilling the promise of the differentiated classroom: Strategies and tools for responsive teaching.* Alexandria, VA: Association for Supervision and Curriculum Development.

Tomlinson, C., & Eidson, C. (2003). *Differentiation in practice.* Alexandria, VA: Association for Supervision and Curriculum Development.

Tomlinson, C., & Strickland, C. (2005). *Differentiation in practice: A resource guide for differentiating curriculum, grades 9–12.* Alexandria, VA: Association for Supervision and Curriculum Development.

Walberg, H., & Uguroglu, M. (1979). Motivation and achievement: A quantitative synthesis. *American Educational Research Journal, 16,* 375–89.

Wheatley, M. (2006). *Leadership and the new science: Discovering order in a chaotic world.* San Francisco: Berrett-Koehler.

Wolfe, P. (2001). *Brain matters: Translating research into classroom practice.* Alexandria, VA: Association for Supervision and Curriculum Development.

Wong, H., & Wong, R. (2007). Teachers: The next generation. *ASCD Express*. Accessed at www.newteacher.com/pdf/ascd_express_wong_teachers.pdf on May 15, 2009.

Wormeli, R. (2006). *Fair isn't always equal: Assessing and grading in the differentiated classroom*. Portland, ME: Stenhouse.

Wormeli, R. (2007). *Differentiation: From planning to practices, grades 6–12*. Portland, ME: Stenhouse.

York-Barr, J., Sommers, W., Ghere, G., & Montie, J. (2001). *Reflective practice to improve schools: An action guide for educators*. Thousand Oaks, CA: Corwin.

Zepeda, S. (2008). *Professional development: What works*. Larchmont, NY: Eye on Education.

Index

Revisiting Professional Learning Communities at Work™
Richard DuFour, Rebecca DuFour, and Robert Eaker
This 10th-anniversary sequel to *Professional Learning Communities at Work™* offers advanced insights on deep implementation, the commitment/consensus issue, and the human side of PLC. **BKF252**

On Common Ground
Edited by Richard DuFour, Robert Eaker, and Rebecca DuFour
Examine a colorful cross-section of educators' experiences with PLC. This collection of insights from practitioners throughout North America highlights the benefits of PLC. **BKF180**

The Collaborative Teacher
Cassandra Erkens, Chris Jakicic, Lillie G. Jessie, Dennis King, Sharon V. Kramer, Thomas W. Many, Mary Ann Ranells, Ainsley B. Rose, Susan K. Sparks, and Eric Twadell
Foreword by Rebecca DuFour
Introduction by Richard DuFour
Transform education from inside the classroom. This book delivers best practices of collaborative teacher leadership, supporting the strategies with research and real classroom stories. **BKF257**

Learning by Doing
Richard DuFour, Rebecca DuFour, Robert Eaker, and Thomas Many
This book demonstrates how collaborative teams can take action to close the knowing-doing gap and transform their schools into professional learning communities. **BKF214**

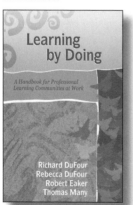

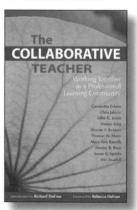